Quõ Vãdis Univer-Cities?

"'Univer-cities' expresses in one word the role that universities now play in their cities and communities. Apart from their traditional role of education and research (the Humboldtian system), one can add a third component which is being a key part of society through the generation of novel employment and start-ups, providing life-long learning and generally interacting with their local communities. Universities have also become exemplars of good practice in developing resilient and sustainable campuses. Now, in our globalised world, apart from their local connections, univer-cities need to stay connected with each other."

Emeritus Professor Bertil Andersson,
Emeritus President NTU,
Nobel Trustee and
Univer-Cities Advisory Councillor

"Now it's 2020. In the midst of a lingering pandemic, we ask ourselves, not for the first time, how to deal with place, space, community, and equity in a univer-city that is both local and global, real and virtual. This time around, our 30-year horizon looks to a new mid-century."

Professor Richard Bender,
Former Professor of Architecture and Dean Emeritus, College of Environmental Design, University of California, Berkeley and Univer-Cities Advisory Councillor

"Like a compass with one leg firmly anchored in the wisdom of the past, this Univer-Cities fourth volume traces a broad arc that is global in its embrace, extending its reach in both space and time to encompass the challenges and uncertainties of the future for which we must responsibly plan."

Dr Roseann O'Reilly Runte,
President and CEO,
The Canada Foundation for Innovation and
IPP-Vice Chancellor, Carleton University

"Universities are the hotbed to produce entrepreneurs of the future. They provide innovations which can lead to commercialisation. With an early in-house angel VC unit, one of our first few NTU start-ups in the 1990s, Nanofilm, is today a breakthrough billion-dollar IPO 'unicorn' which univer-cities should be proud of."

Professor Cham Tao Soon,
Founder President (Emeritus),
Nanyang Technological University and
Univer-Cities Advisory Councillor

"The future will be a conundrum. The entrepreneurs of the future are not different from the entrepreneurs of the past. Each in their time and space. The mentor must be one who has failed and succeeded. The university that radiates from the centre must be one born of successful innovation and successful entrepreneurs."

Edmund Yong ACA,
Founder and CEO,
Xcelerator Fund

"When universities build excellence and engage with partners to fast forward delivery of imagined innovation and impact, governments build confidence in the hybrid role of univer-cities within the economy and communities they serve. Thus while universities can remain proud of their genetic origins it is the 'epigenetic' adaptation that is required if universities are to be well placed to play key leadership roles at times of geopolitical, economic and social disruption."

Professor Dr (Med) Caroline McMillen AO,
Chief Scientist, Government
of South Australia and
IPP-Vice Chancellor, University of Newcastle

"Engaged in this series since UC2013, I am convinced that univer-cities have a vital role to play in global city-driven societies of the future. Their role is to lead our current and next generations in the process of managing and adapting in complex changing-changes, sometimes chaotic world, yet embracing challenges and emerge stronger in solidarity with stakeholders and society."

J. Ong,
Originator, Family Wealth & FinTech Advisors,
Former Executive Director, UBS and Credit Suisse

UNIVER-CITIES

RESHAPING STRATEGIES TO MEET RADICAL
CHANGE, PANDEMICS AND INEQUALITY
REVISITING THE SOCIAL COMPACT?

VOLUME IV

Highly Recommended Titles

Univer-Cities: Strategic Implications for Asia
Readings from Cambridge and Berkeley to Singapore
ISBN: 978-981-4508-65-0 (pbk)

Univer-Cities: Strategic View of the Future
From Berkeley and Cambridge to Singapore and Rising Asia
Volume II
ISBN: 978-981-4630-26-9 (pbk)

Univer-Cities: Strategic Dilemmas of Medical Origins and Selected
Modalities
Water, Quantum Leap & New Models
Volume III
ISBN: 978-981-3238-72-5 (pbk)

UNIVER-CITIES
RESHAPING STRATEGIES TO MEET RADICAL CHANGE, PANDEMICS AND INEQUALITY
REVISITING THE SOCIAL COMPACT?

VOLUME IV

EDITOR

ANTHONY SC TEO

 **World Scientific**

NEW JERSEY · LONDON · SINGAPORE · BEIJING · SHANGHAI · HONG KONG · TAIPEI · CHENNAI · TOKYO

Published by

World Scientific Publishing Co. Pte. Ltd.

5 Toh Tuck Link, Singapore 596224

USA office: 27 Warren Street, Suite 401-402, Hackensack, NJ 07601

UK office: 57 Shelton Street, Covent Garden, London WC2H 9HE

National Library Board, Singapore Cataloguing in Publication Data
Names: Univer-Cities (Conference) (2019 : Singapore), creator. |
    Teo, Anthony S. C., 1944–   editor.
Title: Univer-cities. Volume IV, Reshaping strategies to meet radical change, pandemics and
    inequality : revisiting the social compact? / editor, Anthony SC Teo.
Description: Singapore : World Scientific Publishing Co. Pte Ltd., [2020] |
    Includes bibliographical references and index.
Identifiers: OCN 1226672851 | ISBN 978-981-123-424-8 (paperback)
Subjects: LCSH: Community and college--Congresses. | University towns--Congresses.
Classification: DDC 378.103--dc23

British Library Cataloguing-in-Publication Data
A catalogue record for this book is available from the British Library.

For any available supplementary material, please visit
https://www.worldscientific.com/worldscibooks/10.1142/12207#t=suppl

Desk Editor: Jiang Yulin

Typeset by Stallion Press
Email: enquiries@stallionpress.com

Printed in Singapore

To the idea of the New Silk Roads redefined by univer-cities

CONTENTS

FOREWORD

Alongside the many hardships it has created, the Covid-19 pandemic has also taught us many valuable lessons. Among the most important of these is the urgent need to reconsider some of the existing ways in which we organize our lives and societies. The Univer-Cities project addresses this issue directly in relation to the role of higher education institutions, and the publication of this fourth volume of its work is thus most welcome. Having been present at the inception of this laudable endeavour in 2013, and having followed its evolution since then, I am happy to see that the original focus — on the relationship between universities and the cities in which they are located — is well-represented in this new volume. In this vein, we have new perspectives on this question from the National University of Singapore and the Singapore University of Social Sciences, as well as the University of Berkeley, California. Among other issues, these chapters address the important question of reducing inequalities in the sphere of higher education and beyond. Other contributions take us beyond this core concern, providing insight on topics from expanding access to clean water, to the need for cities to foster greater resilience in the face of the challenges posed by accelerating urbanization and the impacts of climate change.

The importance of collaboration in medical research — addressed at length in the last Univer-Cities volume — is also tackled here, and is of course another issue which has only become more relevant during the pandemic. The unprecedented speed at which effective vaccines have been produced and tested, so crucial to our return to something approaching normalcy, attests to the critical nature of deepening global cooperation in this field. While the institutional, political and other challenges associated with such collaboration should not be minimized, the continued success of projects such as Univer-Cities attests to the potential of the networks created and relationships forged through such efforts. We are living through an undeniably difficult period, but the potential for achieving positive change is also perhaps greater than it has ever been. The Univer-Cities project is an admirable example of such an endeavour, which has allowed some of our most innovative thinkers to pool their considerable collective brain-power in order re-design a better future for us all. The implications of the work collected in this volume go beyond the issues it addresses directly concerning higher education, to encompass this broader human task of re-imagining a world that is better suited to the challenges we now confront.

I want to congratulate all those involved in its publication, and hope that readers will gain as much insight as I have from perusing its contents.

HIS ROYAL HIGHNESS Sultan Nazrin Muizzuddin Shah
The Sultan of Perak
Malaysia
January 2021

FOREWORD

I was happy and honoured to participate in the launchings of Volumes 1 and 3 of Univer-Cities and now look forward to seeing Volume 4 appear.

I am convinced of the impact of this new Volume with its focus on radical changes, changes aimed at reducing inequality, enhancing social compact, and inventing the urgently needed post-pandemic approaches of Univer-Cities.

May I congratulate you, Tony, on this signal achievement.

Rudolph A. Marcus
Nobel Laureate '92
John G. Kirkwood and Arthur A. Noyes Professor of Chemistry
California Institute of Technology
January 2021

ABOUT THE CONTRIBUTORS

Professor Sir Leszek Borysiewicz

Chairman

Cancer Research UK

Former Vice Chancellor

University of Cambridge

Professor Sir Leszek Borysiewicz is a Chair of Cancer Research UK and former Vice Chancellor of the University of Cambridge. He was Chief Executive of the UK's Medical Research Council from 2007, and from 2001 to 2007 was at Imperial College London, where he served as Principal of the Faculty of Medicine and later as Deputy Rector.

As Deputy Rector of Imperial College, Sir Leszek was responsible for the overall academic and scientific direction of the institution, particularly the development of inter-disciplinary research between engineering, physical sciences and biomedicine.

Concurrently with his position at Imperial College, Sir Leszek was also Governor of the Wellcome Trust (2006–2007), Chairman of the UK Clinical Research Collaboration's Integrated Academic Training Awards Panel (2005–2007), and Chair of the HEFCE RAE Main Panel A Assessment Panel.

Sir Borysiewicz was knighted in the 2001 New Year's Honours List for his contribution to medical education and research into developing vaccines, including work towards a vaccine to combat cervical cancer.

Adjunct Professor Anthony SC Teo

Adjunct Professor

School of Business & S R Nathan School of Human Development

Singapore University of Social Sciences

Convenor and Editor

Univer-Cities Conference & Proceedings Volume I-IV

Mr Anthony Teo Soon Chye is Adjunct Professor at Singapore University of Social Sciences. He is a Harvard-trained banker, consultant, business and entrepreneur turned educator, an Emeritus visiting fellow at the University of Cambridge, Wolfson College, and an Emeritus Board Director of HBS Global Alumni Association Board of Directors at Harvard University Graduate School of Business Administration.

He held numerous positions in Nanyang Technological University (NTU), including Chairman of the S$100 million Youth Olympics Games Village 2010 Steering Committee and was a member of the NTU Cabinet in the troika of President, Provost and himself as Secretary to the University and Advisor, and recipient of the NTU Pioneer Educator's Award 2015. He also served on the Board of Greenship Holdings, Subsidiary of Jaccar Holdings of France, SGX-listed InnoValues Limited and latterly as Advisor to Vertical Avis WindFram LLP.

His academic engagement includes lecturing at NTU's Nanyang Technopreneurship Centre, INSEAD's Professor Henri Claude De Bettignies SE Asia Executive Programmes, Munich-based TUM's 'Re-Attracting Overseas German Talent' and Air Liquide Global Senior Executive Development Programme. He was also involved as Panel Chairman for various Panels such as 'Building World Class Universities, QS University Rankings & Asia Pacific Conference' and member of its Conference Academic Committee, conference Provost for Harvard Business School Global Leadership Forum in Hong Kong on Pre-Handover in 1997 and Shanghai on Post-WTO in 2004, besides co-chairman of Univer-Cities Conference 2013, 2016 and 2019 and editor of the proceedings.

Professor Cheong Hee Kiat

President

Singapore University of Social Sciences

Professor Cheong Hee Kiat is Founding President of Singapore University of Social Sciences. He joined academia in Nanyang Technological University in 1986, and held various academic and administrative appointments including Deputy President and Dean of Civil and Environmental Engineering.

He has served on the boards of several tertiary education institutions, the Public Utilities Board and Building and Construction Authority (BCA), and public committees. He has also been active in university accreditation and academic audits in Singapore and internationally. He is currently a member of the NIE Council, the Singapore Engineering Accreditation Board, and chairman of the BCA Academy Advisory Panel. He also chairs the Board of the Singapore Bible College.

Professor Cheong graduated from the University of Adelaide and the Imperial College, London. He is a registered Professional Engineer (Civil) and Fellow of the Institution of Engineers Singapore, the Singapore Academy of Engineers and the Society of Project Managers.

Associate Professor Calvin Chan

Director, Office of Graduate Studies

Singapore University of Social Sciences

Associate Professor Calvin Chan is Director, Office of Graduate Studies, at the Singapore University of Social Sciences. His research concerns the social and organisational aspects of information systems, with particular interest on the digital transformation of the private sector (e.g., digital disruption of SME), public sector (e.g., e-government and smart cities) and people sector (smart communities and Information and Communications Technology [ICT] & Ageing). His research has been published in leading journals and conferences in the Information Systems discipline. He also serves on a number of government committees related to ICT & Ageing. He received his PhD from the National University of Singapore and BSc (Hon) from the University of Warwick.

Professor Tan Eng Chye

President

National University of Singapore

Professor Tan Eng Chye was appointed President of the National University of Singapore (NUS) on 1 January 2018. He is the University's 5th president, and the 23rd leader to head Singapore's oldest higher education institution.

Professor Tan, who attended Raffles Institution (1974–1979), obtained his Bachelor in Mathematics (First Class Honours, 1985) at NUS and his PhD (1989) at Yale University. He joined NUS as a faculty member in the Department of Mathematics in 1985, as a Senior Tutor, and has held visiting positions at various universities overseas such as the Rutgers University, University of Washington at Seattle, University of California at Berkeley and University of Maryland, USA; Universities of Tokyo and Kyoto, Japan; as well as the Hong Kong University of Science and Technology.

Professor Tan's research interests are in the Representation Theory of Lie Groups and Lie Algebras; and Invariant Theory and Algebraic Combinatorics. He has been invited to speak in numerous top conferences overseas, and has published more than 20 articles in top internationally-refereed journals and conference proceedings. He has co-authored three books on mathematics, including a well-known graduate text on non-Abelian harmonic analysis.

Professor Tan is a passionate and award-winning educator. He was a pioneer architect of the current academic system in NUS, and has seeded many initiatives such as the Special Programme in Science, University Scholars Programme, University Town Residential College Programme, Grade-free Year, and Technology-enhanced Education. He was recognised with the University Teaching Award for Innovative Teaching in 1998, and was President of the Singapore Mathematical Society (2001–2005) as well as the South East Asian Mathematical Society (2004–2005).

Professor Tan sits on the International Advisory Council of the Southern University of Science and Technology in China. He is a member of Singapore's Future Economy Council, which is tasked with driving the growth and transformation of the country's future economy. Professor Tan is on the boards of the Agency for Science, Technology and Research (A*STAR); National Research Foundation; and NUS High School of Mathematics and Science. He is a past board member of the Defence Science Organisation (DSO) Laboratories, National Institute of Education, and Infocomm Development Authority of Singapore.

Professor Tan received the Public Administration Medal (Gold) at Singapore's National Day Awards in 2014 for his outstanding contributions to education. He was awarded the Wilbur Lucius Cross Medal, which honours exceptional alumni in the areas of scholarship, teaching, academic administration and public service, by Yale University in 2018. Professor Tan was also conferred an Honorary Doctor of Science from the University of Southampton in 2018 in recognition of his achievements as "an innovative and exceptional teacher, and then as a distinguished and respected leader in academia".

Dr Gordon Johnson

Former President

Wolfson College

Former Deputy Vice Chancellor

Cambridge University

Dr Gordon Johnson is a Cambridge-educated historian. He went up to Trinity College, Cambridge in 1961, and following his first degree, he wrote a PhD thesis on early Indian Nationalism. He was a Fellow successively of Trinity and Selwyn Colleges and then President of Wolfson College. Dr Johnson chaired Cambridge University Press from 1993 until 2009. He edited Modern Asian Studies from 1971 to 2008 and was General Editor of the New Cambridge History of India.

Dr Johnson was Director of the Centre of South Asian Studies in Cambridge from 1983 to 2001. Provincial Politics and Indian Nationalism (CUP, 1973) is the book of his thesis. He has also published a Cultural Atlas of India (1995) and University Politics: F M Cornford's Cambridge and his advice to the young academic politician (CUP, 1994; centenary edition 2008). He is currently writing a book about Cambridge University Press and is past President of the Royal Asiatic Society.

Professor Richard Bender

Former Professor of Architecture and Dean Emeritus

College of Environmental Design, University of California, Berkeley

Professor Richard Bender is the former Dean of the College of Environmental Design and Chair and Professor of Architecture at UC Berkeley.

Ms Emily Marthinsen

Campus Architect and Assistant Vice Chancellor for Physical and Environment Planning emerita

University of California, Berkeley

Campus Architect and former Assistant Vice Chancellor for Physical and Environment Planning, University of California, Berkeley (UC Berkeley), Ms Emily Marthinsen is responsible for campus physical and environment planning. Her portfolio includes project planning and design, sustainability, city and private development partnerships and campus long range development planning.

Ms Marthinsen has a Bachelor of Arts in Geography from the University of Chicago and a Master of Architecture from UC Berkeley. She is a licensed architect in California and has over 35 years of relevant work experience at UC Berkeley and with design and planning firms in Berkeley, San Francisco, Washington, DC, and Alexandria, Virginia.

Ms Marthinsen is a Fellow of the American Institute of Architects (AIA) and a member of the Society for Campus and University Planning and the Association of University Architects. She is past chair of the National AIA's Public Architects Advisory Group, and is a frequent presenter and writer on campus planning issues.

Mr John Parman

Visiting Scholar in Architecture

University of California, Berkeley

Mr John Parman is a Visiting Scholar in Architecture at Berkeley and co-founder of Snowden & Parman, an editorial studio. He is on the editorial and design advisory committee of ARCADE, the Seattle cultural and design quarterly; and is an editorial advisor to Architect's Newspaper; AR&D, ORO Editions' research imprint; and Room One Thousand, an annual edited by graduate architecture students at Berkeley. He and Berkeley Professor Richard Bender cofounded the Urban Construction Laboratory (1989). Mr Parman was the editorial director at Gensler (1997-2017), co-founding its client magazine, Dialogue, in 2000, and launching its Design Forecast in 2013. He cofounded the award-winning quarterly Design Book Review (1983-2002).

Mr Parman has an M.Arch. in Building Technology from U.C. Berkeley, where he was also a doctoral student; and a B.A. in Architecture and History from Washington University.

Professor James Best

President's Chair in Medicine
Dean, Lee Kong Chian School of Medicine

Nanyang Technological University

Professor James Best, a distinguished medical leader who has dedicated his career to improving treatments for diabetes and kidney disease, is Dean of the Lee Kong Chian School of Medicine (LKCMedicine).

Professor Best is formerly the Head of Medical School at the University of Melbourne in Australia, and has 30 years' experience in research, teaching and medical leadership.

A graduate of the University of Melbourne in 1972, Professor Best has practised in the discipline of Endocrinology in Australia, Hong Kong, the USA and the UK. He trained in Endocrinology at Melbourne's St Vincent's Hospital and in diabetes research at the University of Washington, Seattle, USA. Having worked as an Endocrinologist at St Vincent's from 1982 to 1989, he joined the University of Melbourne staff as Deputy Head of the Department of Medicine (St Vincent's Hospital) and in 1999, was appointed as Professor of Medicine and Head of Department. He has also been Deputy Dean of the Faculty from 2004 to 2006 and subsequently Associate Dean (Resources).

In July 2007, he was appointed as Head, Melbourne Medical School (MMS), a School that was established in 1862, and today ranks among the top 20 medical schools worldwide by the Times Higher Education. As Head of School, he was responsible for medical education and for health and medical research involving 23 biomedical science and clinical departments.

Professor Best has taught extensively during his career, especially on the topic of diabetes and metabolism, as well as on the medical interview. His research has involved physiological and molecular studies of glucose disposal, as well as studies of lipid biochemistry and epidemiological and clinical studies of risk factors for cardiovascular disease in diabetes. His current research is predominantly in healthcare delivery for diabetes prevention and management.

Professor Best has been on the Board of Directors of three different Health Services and a Medical Defence Organisation in Australia. He is currently on the Board of St Vincent's Institute (Medical Research) and on the Heart Foundation (Australia) Research Committee. In 2006, he was appointed to the Council of Australia's peak funding body for medical research, the National Health and Medical Research Council (NHMRC), and from July 2006 to June 2012, served as Chair of the NHMRC Research Committee.

The author of over 200 publications, Professor Best is a Fellow of the Royal Australasian College of Physicians, Royal College of Pathologists, Royal College of Physicians of Edinburgh and Honorary MD from St Andrews University.

Professor Frank Rühli

Founding Chair (Full Professor) and Director of the Institute of Evolutionary Medicine

University of Zurich

Frank Rühli, MD, PhD is Founding Chair (Full Professor) and Director of the Institute of Evolutionary Medicine, University of Zurich. He is also currently an Honorary Visiting Professor at the Lee Kong Chian School of Medicine, Nanyang Technological University Singapore; an Honorary Adjunct Professor at the Adelaide Medical School, The University of Adelaide, Australia; and a Distinguished Visiting Professor at the School of Public Health, Tehran University of Medical Sciences, Iran. He is also a member of the Parliament of Zurich and appointed to the Commission of Industrial Enterprises. He has held visiting researcher status at Harvard University and a visiting professorship at the University of Geneva. Professor Rühli is steering committee member of two University Research Priority Initiatives and he is a member of the Medical Faculty and the Science Faculty at the University of Zurich. His main expertise is e.g., the study of evolutionary medicine (including ongoing evolution), anatomy, academic governance and health care policy. Professor Rühli has acquired ca. 17 million USD of third-party funding and has ca. 250 scientific publications. He serves in multiple professional bodies, editorial boards and political organisations (e.g., currently as President, Health Care Commission, Free Democratic Liberal Party Switzerland). Professor Rühli holds also an Executive MBA degree and serves in the rank of a lieutenant-colonel responsible for Medical Scenarios, Headquarter Swiss Army.

Professor Maciej Henneberg

Emeritus Wood Jones Professor of Anthropological and Comparative Anatomy

University of Adelaide

Maciej Henneberg PhD, DSc, FRSB is an Emeritus Wood Jones Professor of Anthropological and Comparative Anatomy in the Adelaide Medical School, University of Adelaide, an Adjunct Professor, Archaeology, Flinders University of South Australia, Visiting Professor in the Institute for Evolutionary Medicine, University of Zurich, Switzerland and an International Fellow of UBVO at the Oxford University, UK.

Born in Poland, he was educated at the Adam Mickiewicz University in Poznan (Biology, Master degree in Human biology, doctorate in physical anthropology and the higher doctorate in anthropology) where he started his academic career as a lecturer. He conducted research on ancient human skeletons and excavated historical cemeteries. He was invited in 1978 to teach at the University of Texas in Austin where he also worked there as the State Archaeologist organising and supervising recovery of Late Archaic American Indian skeletons from the burial ground Loma Sandia in the Live Oak County, Texas.

In 1986 moved to the University of Cape Town, South Africa where he worked as an Associate Professor of Anatomy, but continued collaboration with the Institute of Classical Archaeology, University of Texas excavating and studying Ancient Greek burials in Metaponto, Italy. In 1990 became a Professor and Head of the Department of Anatomy and Human Biology at the University of the Witwatersrand in Johannesburg. His duties included responsibility for the body donation program. Besides excavating burial sites and studying skeletons in South Africa, his continued work in Italy resulted in his, and his wife's (also a human biologist), invitation in 1993 to study human skeletal remains resulting from the eruption of volcano (Vesuvius) in Pompeii. Studies of ancient human skeletons in Italy are continued today.

In 1996 he became the Foundation Wood Jones Professor of Anthropological and Comparative Anatomy at the University of Adelaide.

At the University of Adelaide, he was the Head of the anatomy department from 1997–2009 responsible for the body donation program. He retired in December 2018, but continues academic activities as an Emeritus Professor.

With his 30 PhD students Maciej developed new methods of diagnosing diseases, age and sex from human skeletal remains. Besides studying human skeletal remains, Maciej runs studies of child growth in Indonesia, Africa and Poland, studies of obesity (as the Fellow of the Unit for Biocultural Variation and Obesity, at Oxford), human evolution, especially the evolution of human brain, and the worldwide epidemiology of cancers. Maciej published 5 books, 5 monographs and 400 research papers/book chapters. Maciej appeared as a forensic expert of human identification in courts in Poland, United States of America, South Africa and most jurisdictions in Australia.

Mr Francis Larios

Chief Learning Officer

PHINMA Education

Francis Larios is the Chief Learning Officer of PHINMA Education. His team co-designs and helps improve programs that help their students get in school, finish school, and get a job, whether they finish their schooling or not. He holds a Bachelor of Arts in Social Sciences from Ateneo de Manila University.

Ms Roseanne Agas Ramirez

Writer and Educator

PHINMA Education

Roseanne Agas Ramirez is a writer and educator who joined PHINMA Education in 2019 as a Corporate Communications Specialist. She holds a Bachelor of Arts in Political Science and a Master of Asian Studies from the University of the Philippines Diliman.

Professor Asit K. Biswas

Distinguished Visiting Professor

University of Glasgow

Chairman

Water Management International Pte Ltd

Professor Asit K. Biswas is the founder of the Third World Centre for Water Management in Mexico and Chairman of Water Management International Pte Ltd, Singapore, and currently is a Distinguished Visiting Professor at the University of Glasgow, UK. Formerly a Professor in UK, Canada and Sweden, he was a member of the World Commission on Water. He has been a senior advisor to 19 governments, six Heads of the United Nations Agencies, Secretary General of OECD and also to many other major international and national organisations. He is a Past President of the International Water Resources Association, and has held important positions in several major international water and environment-related professional associations. Professor Biswas is the founder of the International Journal of Water Resources Development and has been its Editor-in-Chief for the past 28 years. He has been the author or editor of 81 books (six more are now under publication) and published over 680 scientific and technical papers. His work has now been translated into 37 languages.

Among his numerous prizes are the two highest awards of the International Water Resources Association (Crystal Drop and Millennium Awards), Walter Huber Award of the American Society of Civil Engineering and Honorary Degree of Doctor of Technology from University of Lund, Sweden, and Honorary Degrees of Doctor of Science from University of Strathclyde, Helsinki University of Technology, and Indian Institute of Technology. Professor Biswas received the Stockholm Water Prize in 2006 for "his outstanding and multi-faceted contributions to global water resource issues", as well as the Man of the Year Award from Prime Minister Harper of Canada, and the Aragon Environment Prize of Spain. In 2012, he was named a "Water Hero of the World" by the Impeller Magazine, and also as one of the 10 thought-leaders of the world in water by Reuters. He is a member of the Global Agenda Council on Water Security of the World Economic Forum. He is regular contributor to many national and international newspapers on resource and development related issues, and also is a television commentator in three continents.

Dr Cecilia Tortajada

Professor

School of Interdisciplinary Studies, University of Glasgow

Former Senior Research Fellow

Institute of Water Policy, Lee Kuan Yew School of Public Policy

Dr Cecilia Tortajada is Professor, School of Interdisciplinary Studies, University of Glasgow, and previously Senior Research Fellow, Institute of Water Policy, Lee Kuan Yew School of Public Policy, Singapore. The main focus of her work at present is on the future of the world's water, especially in terms of water, food, energy and environmental securities through coordinated policies.

She has been an advisor to major international institutions like FAO, UNDP, JICA, ADB, OECD and IDRC, and has worked in countries in Africa, Asia, North and South America and Europe on water and environment-related policies. She is a member of the OECD Initiative in Water Governance.

She is a past President of the International Water Resources Association (2007-2009) and an honorary member of the IWRA. Editor-in-Chief of the International Journal of Water Resources Development, Associate Editor of Water International, member of the Editorial Boards of the Journal of Natural Resources Policy Research, International Journal of Water Governance, Urban Planning and Transport Research Journal, Frontiers in Environmental Science and IWRA (India) Journal, and editor of book series on Water Resources Development and Management of Springer. She is also editor of Springer Briefs on Case Studies on Sustainable Development and on Water Science and Technology; and member of series Advisory Board of Springer Briefs in Earth Sciences, Geography & Earth System Sciences. She is the author and editor of more than 30 books by major international publishers. Her work has been translated into Arabic, Chinese, French, German, Japanese and Spanish languages.

Ms Lauren Sorkin

Acting Executive Director, Global Resilient Cities Network

The Rockefeller Foundation

Ms Lauren Sorkin is Acting Executive Director and is based in Singapore where she leads a global team of interdisciplinary professionals to deliver resilience-building services in cities across six continents. Prior to this, she spent six years working with the Asian Development Bank promoting climate responsive development in the Asia Pacific region. Her assignment included overseeing the development of the ADB's first organisation-wide Climate Change Implementation Plan and corresponding staff development programme. She also served in the ADB Vietnam Resident Mission in Hanoi where she managed the integration of climate resilience into the Bank's $7 billion investment portfolio in country. In addition, she has also worked through the USAID Initiative for Conservation in the Andean Amazon to promote green growth in the region as well as with the USAID Eco-Asia Clean Development and Climate Programme facilitating in-person and virtual knowledge sharing between clean energy experts in China, India, Indonesia, the Philippines, Thailand, and Vietnam.

Ms Sorkin holds a Bachelor of Arts in International Relations from Tufts University and a Master of Science in Environment and Development from the London School of Economics. She is also a certified holistic health counsellor and yoga instructor. She speaks fluent Spanish and Hebrew.

Tan Sri Dr (Med) Sharifah Hapsah

Emerita Professor and former Vice Chancellor

Universiti Kebangsaan Malaysia

Tan Sri Dr (Med) Sharifah Hapsah is Emerita Vice Chancellor of Universiti Kebangsaan Malaysia (UKM), current President of the National Council of Women's Organisations of Malaysia and Senior Consultant in the Prime Minister's Department overseeing the Permata programme. She combines her academic and social activist work in gender equality and child development to strengthen community engagement projects in UKM.

Notable projects include the Centre for Education of the Gifted and Talented, Centre for Empowering Youths-at-risk, the Children's Hospital and Yunus Centre for Social Business. She promotes knowledge and technology transfer for wealth creation and social well-being by nurturing a culture of innovation and entrepreneurship in research, teaching and service in UKM living laboratories across Malaysia. Her latest contribution is a chapter on "Institutional Governance for a Shared Global Engagement Mission" in the GUNI-Higher Education in the World 6 publication entitled 'Towards Socially Responsible Higher Education Institutions, Globally and Locally Engaged'.

Professor Suh Nam Pyo

Ralph E & Eloise F Cross Professor Emeritus

Massachusetts Institute of Technology

Professor Suh Nam Pyo was the 13th and 14th President of Korea Advanced Institute of Science and Technology (KAIST). During his tenure (2006–2013), the worldwide reputation of KAIST was significantly improved; by 2014, KAIST was the second highest ranked university in Asia. In engineering, its worldwide ranking is around 20. In 2016, Reuters ranked it the 6th Most Innovative University in the World.

Professor Suh has spent most of his professional career at Massachusetts Institute of Technology (MIT), where he is the Cross Professor Emeritus. He was the Head of the Department of Mechanical Engineering, MIT. Professor Suh was also the Presidential Appointee in charge of engineering at the U.S. National Science Foundation (NSF). He was appointed to this position by President Ronald Reagan and confirmed by the U.S. Senate.

Professor Suh has received many awards, including the ASME Medal, the General Pierre Nicolau Award of CIRP, the Pony Chung Award, the Inchon Education Award, the Ho-Am Prize for Engineering, the Mensforth International Gold Medal of IEE (UK), the Hills Millennium Award from IED (UK), and the Distinguished Service Award of NSF. He has received nine honorary degrees from universities in four continents. He serves on the boards of universities and industrial firms.

ACKNOWLEDGEMENTS

To all our stalwart collegiate pioneers, my gratitude for their faith in inspiring this univer-cities narrative by completing its fourth volume in its first decade. They are richly represented by the historians' historian Dr Gordon Johnson, the Humboldtian academician and thought leader Bertil Andersson, and peerless engineer-educator, the emeritus MIT Eloise Professor NP Suh whose multi-millionaire Malaysian graduate Hock Tan, CEO of Broadcom, created this chaired professorship in his honour.

Pleasingly, Univer-Cities 2019 hosted with élan by President Dr HK Cheong of the Singapore University of Social Sciences attracted 200 distinguished delegates including three chief scientists: Cambridge physiologist-academician from South Australia; a Malaysian physicist from Germany's chipmaker Siltronics GmbH; and Singapore's first physics-engineer-innovator Chief Defence Scientist. Others included a leading local venture capitalist in the end zone towards a "unicorn" home-run or two; a "bulge" investment banker with social enterprise commitment; and NTU's CFO to name a few. These and others expanded the diversity of our univer-cities community to some fifty multi-disciplinary categories of scholars, public and private officials, and captains of industry.

With grace and thanks to:

HRH Sultan Nazrin PhD (Harvard) for assenting to honour this volume with a Foreword in the tradition of his acclaimed Royal Address at Univer-Cities 2013, Sir Leszek Borysiewicz for his incisive and guiding Keynote Address in continuity from Univer-Cities 2016 at Newcastle, and Senior Minister Tharman Shanmugaratnam for his contextually rich Message to Univer-Cities 2019.

Our colleagues who generously give of their time and expertise to the research phase 2021-2022 with the phrónēsis of Sir Borysiewicz as Patron; ever mindful of Eisenhardt's admonition that case studies can be rich veins to tap into potential theory building and discovery.

Our unsung benefactors who supported our labour of love exemplified by Dr Lee Seng Tee FBA, Chairman of the Lee Foundation, and latterly Lisa Ginsburg for generously granting us the licence to the historic 1922 Einstein in Singapore photograph on his praiseworthy international quest of fundraising for higher education.

My dear Swee Chee at our 51st anniversary and our six grandchildren, Eldest 'Sister' Xuan now at 'O' Levels, Jun, Wen, Yin, Kai, and En in kindergarten. Their grace in sharing my space (as in place-making) in reading, editing and writing is a precious joy. They await my forthcoming 25,000-word *Letter to Grandson Jun*.

Our Group of 10 Advisory Councillors with primus inter pares Nobel Laureate for Chemistry Professor Dr Rudolph Marcus who joyously launched UC Volumes I and III, and a Foreword to Volume IV, my highest esteem and gratitude.

The Team UC2019@SUSS, whose relentless intrepidity is epitomised by differentiated roles of President, Provost and Martin Yuoon, Calvin Chan, Ivy Chua, Nicole Ng and integrated by Vera Lui to seamless effect culminating in an evening to remember at the centennial Clifford Pier restored with its art-deco ambience replete with a man-made reflecting Marina Lake, best under the light of November's moon.

My publishers World Scientific Publishing Company from Founder Professor Dr KK Phua to Max Phua, Chua Hong Koon and YL Jiang, complemented by NTU research librarian Samantha Ang on citations and award winning Resident Artist and Sculptor Yeo Chee Kiong's original cover design in convergence with the narrative, for their unstinting support in this perfect serenity of Univer-Cities Series Volumes I–IV — strategic implications, to strategic view of the future, dynamics of medical origins, and reshaping strategies to meet radical technological, economic, pandemic and social compact disruptions.

Anthony SC Teo
Adjunct Professor
School of Business & S R Nathan School of Human Development
Singapore University of Social Sciences

KEYNOTE ADDRESS

The purpose of universities is to contribute to society through the pursuit of education, learning, and research at the highest levels of excellence. How universities do this individually varies according to time and place. Inevitably, each university develops its own concerns and specialities, but in a world that is increasingly connected, and one experiencing major economic and political disruptions, it is important, as each plays to their own strengths, to be able to see the bigger picture; to realise how our special interests benefit from knowing what happens elsewhere; and to be aware that what we do has implications for others. Research and discovery inform teaching and learning; new knowledge is applied for social and economic benefit, often in unpredictable and unexpected ways; and people should be offered education to enable them to make informed and responsible decisions about their own lives and about society at large. A moral imperative, driving what we do, is to work for the good of all, to be socially inclusive, and to rid society of unjust inequalities.

In our present condition, many of the major challenges facing us in securing a rich and fulfilling life for everyone — climate change, the management of natural resources, the provision of shelter, clean water and food, health care, economic changes and technological innovation — are beset with divisions and exclusions. There is already sufficient evidence to show that access to education and medical care is shot through with inequality; that the rapid economic growth of the last fifty years has increased rather than moderated the distribution of wealth; and that many of the poorer peoples and regions consistently bear the brunt of natural disasters and socio-economic disruptions.

The Univer-Cities project contributes to a necessary debate about how to define, understand and set about finding solutions to these problems. It has based its discussions on case studies and has, in the published papers, drawn out from them ideas to stimulate further thinking. The first two volumes in this series looked at how, in recent decades, the

xli

development of physical infrastructure and educational purposes in Berkeley, Cambridge, Hong Kong, Singapore and elsewhere have met new needs for research and teaching. In addition, they have studied the impact of such dynamic centres of higher education on their respective local, national and international hinterlands. The third volume, which arose from a meeting at Newcastle University, New South Wales, Australia three years ago, focused on the exciting though volatile developments taking place in the fields of bio-medicine — things that straddled pure laboratory work and the crossing of conventional disciplinary boundaries, the training of health specialists, the application of intellectual capital to the development of new drugs and medical procedures, the investment required to bring things together, and the public policy issues that work to ensure a degree of fairness in the outcomes. These are big issues and are far from being satisfactorily resolved. We have a moral duty to future generations to continue to work as creatively and collaboratively as possible to find a way through.

This year's meeting will explore how university towns and cities, and the diverse countries in which they are situated, can best prepare for educating citizens who will understand and contribute to public debate and policy-making; how they can, through continuous learning and professional development, contribute to maintaining a highly skilled workforce competent to tackle global problems; how they can promote sustainable economic growth; and, above all, how what they do removes obstacles to access and mitigates inequality — all with the over-riding purpose of ensuring good and satisfying lives for everyone.

Singapore, with its internationally renowned and complementary universities, rich experience in networking locally, regionally and internationally, is an ideal place to begin driving these debates forward. I am sorry not to be able to be with you in person for what promises to be a vibrant discussion, but I look forward to reading the collected papers in volume IV of the Univer-Cities series of publications.

Sir Leszek Borysiewicz
Former Vice Chancellor, University of Cambridge
and Chairman, Board of Trustees, Cancer Research UK

MESSAGE

Technological advances and digitalisation bring increasing challenge to labour markets globally. They also present opportunities in every society. Our task, in education, life-long learning, and in developing new social norms, must be to enable people in all walks of life to take advantage of these opportunities, and to avoid a divide between digital haves and have-nots. Universities will have to evolve, and remain central to this ecosystem of learning. They play key roles, not only in our investments in the young but in providing opportunities for people to keep growing through life. The Univer-Cities Conference is an important platform for academic, government and industry leaders from around the world to share insights and discuss this evolving role of universities. I wish you a fruitful conference.

Tharman Shanmugaratnam
Senior Minister and Coordinating Minister for Social Policies

CHAPTER ONE

UNIVER-CITIES VOLUME IV: DECADE OF DELIBERATION & QUŌ VĀDIS RESEARCH

ANTHONY SC TEO

"Truth is a pathless land"
J. Krishnamurti

As Convenor and Editor of this univer-cities narrative, I am honoured by the ongoing conversation with our distinguished academic leaders, universities and univer-cities, authors, diverse stakeholders, and our respected Advisory Councillors who have participated in reaching this milestone.

I propose to review UC2019, the fourth in the series on Univer-Cities, in the evolving context of the earlier three. In addition, I will provide a commentary on the significance of the serial contributions and the future differentiating features of the univer-cities of Cambridge and Berkeley.

For perspective, as Convenor and Editor, I deeply appreciate this opportunity to personally welcome the academe's community of scholars and friends for the dialogue to share this update to Volume IV.

In the spirit of enquiry and dialogue, the univer-cities narrative is open-ended, frank and civil, surfacing potentially three dozen cases with differing dimensions. For UC 2019, we met in Singapore at the Singapore University of Social Sciences (SUSS), three Higher Education milestones that took place over the period 1920–2020 are worthy of note, namely:

Milestone 1: *Centennial (1920–2020) Global Context*

THEN: In about 1922 Pioneer Singaporean Sir Manasseh Meyer gave US$25,000 to the pre-cursors of the National University of Singapore (NUS) and another US$25,000 to the Hebrew University of Israel through the personal fund-raising visit of our humanity's pre-eminent scientist of all time, Albert Einstein. He stayed with friends in Singapore as told by a visiting distinguished lecturer Dr Eugene Kandel and with good fortune through the sleuth work of Ambassador Bilahari, we located the owner-licensor Lisa Ginsburg (whose grandfather Charles Ginsburg stood behind Elsa Einstein) who generously granted us the license to publish this exclusive photograph citing 'the impressive Univer-Cities conference and publication' (Figure 1.1).

NOW: Today — both the NUS and Hebrew University are their countries' leading universities.

Einstein's genius casts a long shadow of grace upon the innovation-driven Hebrew University of Jerusalem which is the leading university in Israel. So it is with the centennial National University of Singapore in Singapore — bonus of being joint 11th with youthful 30-year-old NTU by 2019 QS World University Rankings.

Fig. 1.1. Sir Albert Einstein with the Frankel-Clumeck Family, Sir Manasseh Meyer's Estate, Singapore, November 2, 1922. (Image courtesy of the Frankel-Clumeck Family.)

The standing of the NUS is further accelerated by the latent under-lying "Singapore School of Strategic Governance (SS-SG)". This was best expounded in the Harry J. Johnson 3rd Memorial Lecture'83 at the Royal Society by our then Deputy Prime Minister and Minister for Education Dr Goh Keng Swee in the Singapore context of Five-Multi-Merits where we are enjoined to co-exist with dilemmas of the inclusive "*and*" as distinct from the binary "*or*": multi-cultural, multilingual, multi-religious, multi-national and multi-disciplinary.

Milestone 2: Case Setting — "Education Incubator Singapore (SG)"

A descriptive case of Singapore is documented in — *Univer-Cities Volume I: Strategic Implications for Asia. Readings from Cambridge and Berkeley to Singapore* in the chapter "Conversations in Futures of Univer-Cities in the Asia-Pacific: Singapore — Place and Education in the 21ˢᵗ Century".

A sub-theme describes the shaping of "the higher education incubator — Singapore". The chapter was authored by Hal Guida & Andrew Donnelly, Architects and Campus Planners. They brought their experience in dealing with higher education in America, Australasia and in Singapore with NTU, directly engaging its Cabinet (President Su, Provost Andersson & COO Teo) and academic leaders with input from Berkeley's peerless advisor Dr Richard Bender. Working in participative ways through extensive consultations with stakeholders, the outcome was the co-created two-decade place-making vision of the Nanyang Technological University in a (Yunnan) Garden in the context of the university, in Jurong City, Singapore Garden City and State.

Short: The shortest three-point speech known to me was made by US Ambassador George Ney (Reagan & Bush Senior's Presidential Advisor extraordinaire) in the week before the 1991 Deliverance of the Kuwait "Operation Desert Storm". In 10 words, he said simply: "There will be a war. It's short. We'll win. Questions?"

Long: But this chapter is an ongoing narrative, a process of review within a contextual prism.

Milestone 3: *Fourth UC2019 Connecting the Original Mini-Colloquium 2010, UC2013, UC2016 & Quō Vādis 2020*

1. Origin of UC Narrative

The original mini-colloquium was documented in the five papers published in *Univer-Cities Volume I Strategic Implications for Asia*. It was at the conclusion of my Visiting Fellowship at Cambridge when the then Deputy Vice-Chancellor and concurrently President of Wolfson College Dr Gordon Johnson asked me, "What now?" For the love of Cambridge and in my moment of weakness, I said, "I will start a new *urbi et orbi* narrative envisioning the evolving and changing symbiotic nature of univer-cities and drawing on Cambridge's 800-year evolution from a monastic university with a modest medieval market town to global pre-emption with, amongst others, multi-billion Silicon Valley (or Silicon Fen with a phenomenal research-innovation eco-system that turned out an exemplary US$35 billion ARM-chip that powers the ubiquitous mobility devices, and fast disrupted the PC-based Intel-chips)."

Dr Gordon Johnson, the historians' historian smiled and before he could say another word, I requested, "May it please you to be the First UC Advisory Councillor?" At UC2019 we had ten. Present were Dr Gordon Johnson, NTU Founder President Professor Cham Tao Soon, MIT Emeritus Eloise Professor, NP Suh via Zoom, Emerita UKM VC Tan Sri Dr (Med) Sharifah Hapsah, Berkeley Dean Emeritus Richard Bender (represented by serial co-authors Emerita DVC Marthinsen & Visiting Scholar Parman in Volume I–IV) and Nobel Trustee & IPP NTU Professor Bertil Andersson through his colleague NTU-ICL Lee Kong Chian School of Medicine (LKCSM) Dean Dr (Med) James Best.

2. Now — Four in the UC Series

The inaugural Univer-Cities mini-colloquium was documented in the publication of UC Volume I in 2013 titled *Univer-cities: Strategic Implications for Asia*. The ensuing second cycle UC2013 focused on *Univer-Cities: Strategic View of the Future. From Berkeley and Cambridge to Singapore and Rising Asia* published in 2015. There is an ever present danger confronting new narratives. In the case of Sir Richard Attenborough when he started his crusade on climate change some 60 years ago, some thought it was quirky even cranky. We're luckier. Our Advisors and Colleagues kept us focused, gaining legitimacy.

Our third, UC2016's central theme was, do univer-cities with Medical School origins make them more dynamic and different? It was hosted to much acclaim by medical and healthcare research-intensive Newcastle University, Australia, led by Cambridge trained physiologist Professor Dr (Med) Caroline McMillen.

Centennial NUS-SG seems an added exemplar as the world's 4th most international university by QS 2019 rankings with a tradition of respected medical leaders like the 19th NUS Professor Dr (Surgeon) Lim Pin and Wellcome Trust Scholar-Researcher Professor Dr (Med) Tan Chorh Chuan, presently, Singapore's healthcare czar who cut his teeth as Chief Medical Officer in combatting SARS 2003 before his appointment as 22nd NUS Vice-Chancellor (aided in the prescient build-up of the National Centre for Infectious Diseases [NCID] "ready" for COVID-19 and a 330-bed purpose-built facility for treatment and prevention, that opened in autumn 2019).

An engineering focus of NTU-SG is the more recent strategic-oriented mission of the Lee Kong Chian School of Medicine. Lee Kong Chian School of Medicine (LKCSM) in SG-UK linkage with Imperial College is a later evolution with LKCSM's centennial Tropical-Disease forte teaching hospital. The teaching of medicine at Cambridge in fact dates back to 1540 when Henry VIII endowed the University's first Professorship in Physic, Dr John Blyth. Their Emeritus 345th Vice-Chancellor Professor Dr (Med) Sir Leszek Borysiewicz is now Chairman of the Board of Trustees of Cancer Research UK co-existing with a well-funded Dr Li Kashing Cancer Research Institute at the mammoth Cambridge Bio-Medical Campus.

Forebodingly, Pulitzer Prize honoured scientist turned journalist Ms Laura Garrett knew the then weighty price Singapore had paid for battling SARS 2003 (recording 238 infections and 33 deaths). SARS was fought with mission driven efficiency, protocols and governance in not only improving infection control in the hospital and health services but also on socio-political trust building from the grassroots up to research-ers and professional medical practitioners at the institutions of higher learning and their associated teaching hospitals (centennial Singapore General Hospital and the tropical disease specialty Tan Tock Seng Hospital). Garret apocalyptically warned, "So now they're being put to the test. If Singapore can't do it, if Singapore can't keep it under control, then we're all screwed, because they've got the best system in the world" (Garrett 2020).

COVID-19 is a new strain with many unknowns and the jury is still out. Nevertheless, the evolving bio-medico professionalism and research underpinned by an underlying 50-year practised governance (since DPM's 1983 Royal Society's 3rd Memorial Harry Johnson Lecture) made Singapore the gold standard in fighting SARS 2003 and now, ensuring a low death toll in this ubiquitous global pandemic of COVID-19.

3. Dynamic Disruptive Disequilibrium

UC2019 embraced and deliberated the constant alignment to the dynamic disruptive disequilibrium of economic and global restructuring, technological changes, unsustainable inequality impacting the prevailing social compact and the unexpected COVID-19 pandemic.

Inequality Action Direct

UC IV in 2019 was so fortunate to be hosted by the Singapore University of Social Sciences (SUSS) whose major mission is to deal directly with this needed alignment. With good fortune, Harvard-trained Ramon Del Rosario Jr, Patron of PHINMA Group 1956 (and former Philippines' Minister for Finance), has disruptively innovated the PHINMA Education Network to combat poverty and inequality by "serving determined and resilient youth from low-income families". The record will show affordability, accessibility and quality with enrolment of about 50,000 and growing, principally in IT & Nursing with enviably high employability. Francis Larios, PHINMA Chief Learning Officer, said, "We hope to contribute to President Duterte's army of 10,000 frontline health aides." Admirably, they are poised for Southeast Asian expansion into Indonesia and Myanmar which could derive complementary competitive advantage by adopting and adapting the curated SUSS distance learning capabilities. Francis Larios shared with us the processes, practical yet frugal, in his exposition of "The PHINMA Way in Six Univer-cities from Manila to Iloilo to Cebu City".

Globally univer-cities, however, have not escaped being blind-sided by the scope and pent-up knowable factors, even amongst the Ivy League, as elitist with outliers like MIT and Harvard endowed beyond compare by as much as US$40 billion — larger than the nominal GDP of many countries! The COVID-19 pandemic closed down cities and universities — even Harvard President and his spouse Adele tested positive for the virus and were quarantined. Even if the Corona virus is virulent, with our advances in science and the human condition it is unlikely to be worse than the catastrophic Medieval Black Plague that caused the death of cities, counties and millions. History recounts that Cambridge, Oxford, Bologna and Paris survived and thrived to the 21st Century.

Univer-Cities: Unit of Analysis & Evolutionary Dynamics

Professor Dr (Med) Frank Rühli (Dean of Evolutionary Medicine, University of Zurich) contributed a chapter viewing univer-cities beyond a unit of analysis to the realm of the applicability of an *evolutionary discipline* into further understanding its dynamics. Together with his colleague, Professor Marciej Henneberg of the University of Adelaide, he added some takeaways of the Spanish Flu pandemic of 1918.

Univer-Cities & Widening Resilient Cities

We extended the understanding of univer-cities with the Rockefeller Foundation study of '100 Resilient Cities'. The conversation could benefit from the global set of cities with respect to their own univer-cities dynamics ranging from "Uni'ver-city" to "Duo'ver-city" as in Ottawa-Carleton, to "Tri'ver-city" as in Berkeley, San Francisco and Palo Alto as expounded in UC Volume III. The Rockefeller resilient cities data can be accessed as indicated in the chapter by UKM Emerita Professor Tan Sri Dr (Med) Sharifah.

Univer-Cities & Singular Factor of Water

Stockholm Water Award Winner Professor Dr Asit Biswas and Professor Cecilia Tortajada exceeded themselves with a completely new paper outlining their expert global outlook (including the developed world in locations stretching from Ontario, Milwaukee, and Flint to Singapore) on clean water, before and after COVID-19, and their views of the future. Insouciantly, they quoted Lord Byron who wrote a century ago —

"Till taught by pain,
Men really know not what good
water's worth."

Of the univer-city of Singapore, they commended, "the public-private partnership of thought and long-term plan, often for some 40–50 years; and updated every five years based on new developments, advances in knowledge and technology and additional value of information. We've advised some two dozen countries over the past 50 years. There is absolutely no question that all the Singaporean Ministers we have had the pleasure and privilege to interact with including Minister Mentor Lee are in a class by themselves."

The Singapore case of being water-stressed moving towards water independence is only part of the narrative. The Vatican's Pontifical Academy of Sciences in February 2017 invitation to a colloquium followed on the paper by Biswas and Tortajada to UC2016 at Newcastle, in salutary moments captured in Figures 1.2 and 1.3. This year saw the issuance of the encyclical of Pope Francis, *Fratelli Tutti*. In it is the humanity of water sharing in the midst of inequality of water endowment. The authors' coverage of this inequality noted competing interests for water-sharing as in Malaysia-Singapore, Mekong-Indochina states, Capetown and the Republic of South Africa, Jordan River and the Levant, Colorado-California and the Federated Provinces of Canada, amongst others.

There is a mention in Pope Francis' 2020 Encyclical (Francis 2020):

"Those who enjoy a surplus of water yet choose to conserve it for the sake of the greater human family have attained a moral stature that allows them to look beyond themselves and the group to which they belong. How marvellously human!" (Francis 2020, 117).

The combination of the universities and the city (state) turns out to be a suitable focus to show the dimensions of the multi-faceted Singapore

Fig. 1.2. Stockholm Water Awardee Dr Biswas meets Pope Francis.

School of Strategic Governance (SS-SG) alluded to at the beginning of this chapter. The focus is on the dynamics of action plans to deal with the enormity of this challenge to an island water-stressed community and economy. It is significant to note the continuum of multi-disciplinary to trans-disciplinary approaches to defeat the problem(s) through participatory engagement of multiple stakeholders, expertise and diplomacy. In sync, water & environment are highly endowed research and innovation missions at both NUS & NTU. Both these universities are hosted by a city within an island eco-system with a diverse population of about five million engaging in massive global trade (vis-à-vis its GDP) and growing industry hub operations. Singapore is now approaching the pacific zone of water independence.

A cautionary note on SS-SG: it is not compliance oriented. Its governance is in the mode of strategy, implementation and review. It was originally focused on formulating a new theory of economic development that

Fig. 1.3. Buona Sera Dr Tortajada, Third World Centre for Water Management's Co-Founder.

works not only in theory but in the reality of the power of practice. It is postulated with a needed and necessary input of management (ethics and entrepreneurship) and organs of state to ensure the proper administration and review of formulated economic development plans into realisation. It was grounded and based on the first twenty years of Singapore's 50 years of development from Third World to First World. It embraced inter- to trans-disciplinary thinking as Dr KS Goh was an eminent economist, sociologist, statistician, politician, educator, writer, soldier and ever an originalist who once said, "Why can't a Minister of Government be wrong!" It was a revealing retort to his Permanent Secretary who claimed Dr Goh changed his own mind on a contentious matter at hand — it doesn't matter whether it be technological or organisational choices to defeat problems.

COVID-19 on the other hand expounds SS-SG more clearly in the primacy of process (wearing masks and social distancing matter, testing, immediacy of treatment, and isolation). This is in addition to the other worldly needs of personal protective equipment (PPE) and associated healthcare assets (such as hospitals, ICU, quarantines, treatment protocols, etc.) as well as innovations called for in higher education as you will see in the chapters by the presidents of NUS and SUSS.

4. *Post-COVID: Social Distancing & New Innovations*

SUSS's forte for distance learning has paid dividends. With a full suite, a blending of the physical with the virtual and/or full-online interactions are "delivered on an anytime-any-place mobile-enabled basis". The SUSS learning systems had already been described in UC Volume III. However, with the global spread of the black swan COVID-19 pandemic, few universities have been exempt from offering online learning. SUSS is ready to share their experience and technology to enable a smooth transition in teaching and learning and — fast forward — to the inexorable end-of-semestral assessments.

NUS President has hastened their readiness to assist graduates and industry in light of the far reaching impact of COVID-19, essentially compressing "two years' worth of digital transformation in two months", according to Microsoft CEO Satya Nadella. NUS is availing itself of Singapore's Research, Innovation and Enterprise (RIE) 2020 plan for national R&D efforts, a commitment of S$19 billion for the period 2016–2020. The chapter on NUS cites the elusive pay-off: in 2002–2017 a one per cent increase in R&D stock in a firm led to a 0.135 per cent increase in productivity. This is pleasing as productivity effects are seemingly less elusive. However, we have to take a holistic view applying Total Productivity Factor (TPF) assaying both labour and capital.

This is highlighted in the Harvard Business School's case study of Singapore Inc which was first documented in the late 1970s and recently updated by Professor Richard Veitor. It behoves the univer-city to explore trans-disciplinary approaches just as NUS President Tan asserts.

His commitment is to — strategic positioning to support near-term recovery and engage in longer-term priorities that enable broad (deep) advancement. How? Focused education, research, and innovation and enterprise in the face of shorter job tenures and a limited shelf life for skills and knowledge.

His chapter covers upskilling of alumni using a multi-disciplinary approach but I would like to touch on his strategy of nurturing intellectual versatility. There are two significant vector delta initiatives in the creation of the College of Humanities (through a collegiate collaboration between the Faculty of Science and the Faculty of Social Science) and the university-wide commitment to multi-disciplinary studies.

In essence, that delta leap, as expounded by MIT's Professor Suh at UC2016, must "transform to leap frog to be on a higher trajectory". UC Volume II dealt with the univer-cities' challenge as seminally asserted by Kagan (2009) in praise of the third culture of "Humanities" in addition to Natural Sciences and Social Sciences. Additionally, multi-disciplinary approaches must transverse to trans-*discipline-arity* as many problems and discoveries are found in-between or inter-spatial betwixt the disciplines as he poignantly says "because the most promising breakthroughs happen at the intersection of two or more disciplines". So said our UC Councillor Nobel Laureate Rudolph Marcus of his Marcus Theory which enables the iPhone and similar indispensable gadgets to seamlessly converge multi-data, multi-media and multi-5G simply by physical touch. This is well expounded in the book edited by Gibbons et al. (1994) — NTU conferred on Professor Nowotny, one of the editors, an honorary doctorate of letters towards the end of the 20th century.

These two vector deltas together with NUS' commitment to a transformative residential liberal arts college education through their Yale-NUS College is a tri-lateral focus that will help re-define post-COVID NUS towards the promise of a premier univer-city of Singapore that dove-tails organisational development in its academic, research and financial architecture. In a discussion with the Provost Professor Dr 'Teck' Ho, an accomplished teacher, researcher and thought leader from Berkeley, we visited the yonder — beyond the community of scholars and towards the ultimate of a self-renewing *society of scholars* (SS) if it could be akin to the acronym SJ (Society of Jesus), the jesuitical defenders of the faith. The reason is that more is expected of those who aspire to the rare "exemplar twelve" apostles or the Top 12 Universities Globally amongst 10,000. To be sure, universities must contend with novel institutions and ideation like the World Economic Forum whose founder Klaus Schwab was conferred an NUS honorary doctorate.

NTU is remarkable for its successful medical school graduating its dually qualified NTU-Imperial College of London doctors employable in the UK and in Singapore, with its much in demand tropical disease forte. NTU has bolstered its leadership with an MIT-Carnegie Mellon appointment of its third president Professor Dr Subra Suresh; and the former Cambridge Vice-Chancellor Sir Borysiewicz as Trustee who notably spearheaded the outstanding search and hiring of Professor Dr (Med) Joseph Sung following the latter's vice-chancellorship of the respected Chinese University of Hong Kong (CUHK) which incidentally is the eastern "univer-city home" to Physics Nobel Laureate CN Yang and the late Economics Laureate Sir James Mirlees. Blending NTU's core Engineering with Humanities, it is now refreshing the original remit to be more global in its medical education, teaching and research — propitiously creating a vaunted vector delta.

Unsustainable Inequality

In addressing the issue of combating unsustainable inequality and revisiting the social compact, my preference is first to deal with the issues of "contract or compact" and then the matter of revisiting it.

Contract or Compact: After comparing the prevalence of these two terms in the literature using Google Books Ngram Viewer, as of November 16, 2020, 'Social Contract' expounded by Rousseau, Locke, Mills et al. claims the lead (see Figure 1.4). Contemporary mores envisioned a broader social compact framing the social experiment of the 17th century Jamestown settlement. Unfortunately, it highlighted the joint stock company shareholder-centric and it has been a long struggle to bring back in focus the present-day broader-based range of stakeholders.

In a social capital lecture to Singapore NGO leaders, Carl Schramm, former Kauffman Foundation's president, revisited his 600-city review and the case for enterprise of an entrepreneurial kind as a distinguishing

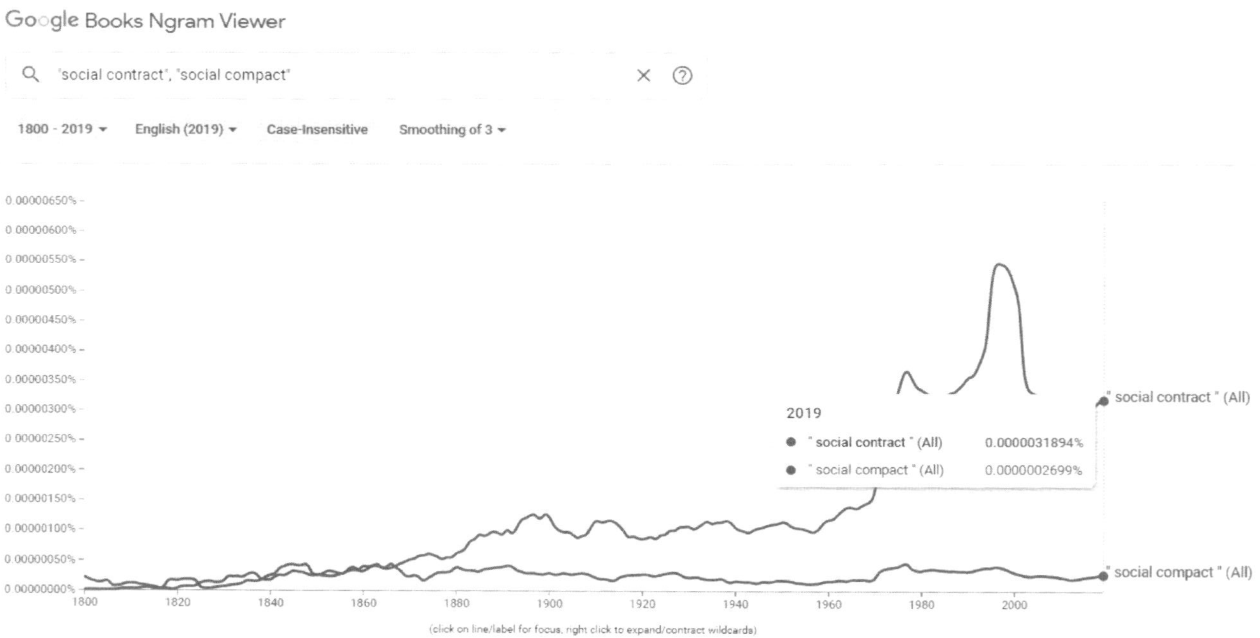

Fig. 1.4. Usage of "social contract" and "social compact" in Google Books corpus (English 2019).

Note: This Ngram shows the occurrence of these two concepts, social contract and social compact, from 1800s to present day. Available from: Google Books Ngram Viewer https://books.google.com/ngrams, accessed November 16, 2020. Screenshot by author.

success feature (repeated often in the addresses of the 23rd NUS President Tan and Emeritus MIT Eloise Professor Suh).

My attention was drawn to Genoa. Genoa in the 13th century was a pre-eminent city-state rivalling Venice. Genoa with its financial prowess (akin to our sovereign wealth funds) had overseas Mediterranean possessions through Italy, Greece and the "Crusader States". Yet the "social contract" between the city's family-clans and its self-enforcing governance system frayed into disarray. The clans jointly outsourced the city's administration through the hiring of a third party "military podesta" (Greif 1998) helped for a further spurt of mutual cooperation without morphing the administrating cum mediating podesta to become a dictator before the breakdown of Genoa's self-enforcing governance system. Now, the rest is history. Today, Genoa is best known as a tourist destination and came into the spotlight recently for the infamous collapse of an aging highway aqueduct-bridge.

Narrow versus Broader Origins: In applying the origins of (social) compact, I prefer this broader terminology. The contextualists and textualists point to the original documents like the Constitution of the United States. Many countries such as the United Kingdom, however, do not have written constitutions. Some refer to key speeches of pioneer country leaders Pierre Elliot Trudeau or Minister Mentor Lee Kuan Yew for the concise words — "More just and equal society".

Social Compact: It is defined as giving "expression to and is based on the reciprocal ties that hold families, governance, and society together over time. When humanely conceived and honoured at each level, the compact has fostered and remains necessary for human development and progress" (Cornman, Kingson, and Butts 1998, 10–11). Further clarity injected by former US Secretary of Labour Robert Reich reminds us that "we" are "all in this together" and former Social Security Commissioner Robert Ball adds that "we" are the present "with debts to the past and obligations to the future" (11). I am partial to the views of SUSS's President Cheong who in his chapter introduced the United Nations Sustainable Development Goals (SDG). These 17 SDGs are like KPIs (with the attendant limits of any KPI). Cheong establishes the cogent argument of the centrality of his tertiary UC mission of up-skilling and re-skilling (4th SDG) to addressing multiple but related issues of Decent

Work & Economic Growth (8th), Reduce Inequalities (10th), Good Health & Well-Being (3rd), Gender Equality (5th), Industry, Innovation & Infrastructure (9th) and Sustainable Cities & Communities (11th).

The 17 SDGs are descriptive with underlying prescriptive features (International Council for Science 2017). For example, the "10th SDG on Reducing Inequalities" includes a condition that needs curing and improvements rather than just relying on a single factor GINI coefficient.

A reading of the regular UN Annual Reports makes for instructive ongoing "performance reviews" whether it be of the United States of America or the city state of Singapore. In context, the reviews provide an overall picture yet with some granularity and potential triangulation to connected goals. They indicate common factors and potential causality for envisioning human development and progress.

NUS President Tan has also pointed to the impact of COVID-19 on inequality and the social economic divide in particular. The disproportionate impact on COVID-19 on those members of society least able to absorb disruption or dislocation has brought these longstanding tensions to the fore, highlighting the frayed social compact in many developed countries. Interestingly, the importance of the United Nation's Sustainable Development Goals encompassing objectives such as reducing inequality, and encouraging economic growth for wider prosperity is noted.

Governance, Access & Affordability: A social compact includes the issues of governance, while the pandemic raises the mortality risks as expressed in the issue of equality of access to vaccines. A univer-city must keep its inner innovative and research eyes on affordability and equality of access as asserted by Sir Borysiewicz in his address at UC2016 reported in UC Volume III. This point was re-emphasised by Newcastle's Laureate Professor Aitken who laid out the needed "Aitken factor" to re-align univer-city research with a nuevo social impact, thus re-framing the implicit social compact instead of pure research. Such re-alignment would be befitting of radical "Newcastrian" innovations from coal to steel to city renewal through the creation of new clusters in higher education of jurisprudence with moot courts and facilities connected to the real life law courts and its eco-system of the legal profession. Added to these are the new enterprise creations with applied entrepreneurial learning and proto-typing. There would also be adjacent access to meditation-arbitration for Newcastle's nearby Hunter Valley wineries and regional healthcare services.

Revisiting: An approach of this nature — encompassing governance, access and affordability — could more readily engage the revisiting of the existing social compact. They may also serve as pointers to encourage societies to reinforce their core and secondary values toward a renewed and emergent social compact anchored within the greater society that univer-cities serve.

Univer-cities of Berkeley & Cambridge: The activist contributors are sagely Cambridge historian Dr Gordon Johnson and place-making architect, design and environmentalist Dr Richard Bender. The evidence is telling — the mega Cambridge Bio-Med campus with its "College self-enforcing" innovation-driven Silicon Fen phenomenon and its Nobel accolades are self-evident recognition. Berkeley engages its city more radically from the armature of Berkeley's operating campus planning study group aligned to the strategic long-range development plans that increasingly develop a shared role and fate like a univer-city. The Zuckerberg-Chan $3 billion initiative for better healthcare impact (without any increment to mortar assets) asserted the nuclear case towards a collective "Tri'ver-city" compact comprising Berkeley with the University of San Francisco and Stanford at Palo Alto. Conceptually, the optimism of the Morrill Act 1862 created the rising Berkeley bar with respect in multi-fields. The moniker carpark lot for the next Nobel Laureate is reflective of the "3 on 3 rivalry" Nobel awards between MIT, Berkeley and CalTech vis-à-vis Harvard, Cambridge and Oxford dominance. Bender thinks aloud, alluding to the university's "long clock" with longer institutional memory and time to reflect on the desirability of the "big ideas". The imaginary vision of a comparable "Nuevo Morrill Act 2020" animates the envisioning of the new Athens of the Univer-city of Berkeley.

Bender Proposition: Bender reasserts the premise of "*the univer-city as an alternate model*" — seedbed and laboratory, akin to the Guida proposition of Singapore as an incubator, where "place and community transform each other" through higher education.

Quō Vādis — Research

The three dozen UC cases are studies of the potential theorems, alternative plan(s) of action ahead and the basic UC Mix (like the breakthrough *Marketing Mix* of HBS Professor Neil Borden whom I brought to Singapore some 50 years ago together with strategy Professor Ram Charan, presently Citibank Advisor, and the late Management Control Systems Professor Warren Haynes). Public administrators have Public Policy Schools like the Harvard Kennedy School of Government and Singapore's Lee Kuan Yew School of Public Policy (LKY-SPP). Where do aspiring academics go to ready themselves for thought and vice-chancellor leadership whilst existing amongst their community or society of scholars? Cambridge makes their own timber in its 800-year history with 345 VCs including Sir Borysiewicz or an average of 2.35 years of inter-linked (Rector and Regent-in-Waiting) continuity beyond founding faith and mission — the most Nobel laureates per acre in academe's hallowed little acre!

Quō Vādis — Research Oversight

In the spirit of collegiality, the structure of the UC IV research has been threefold:

(a) *Strategic Oversight* of UC Councillor Professor Dr Bertil Andersson, UC Councillor Former Cambridge Deputy VC Dr Gordon Johnson & MIT Emeritus Professor Dr Nam Pyo Suh,

(b) *Operational Supervision* of NUS President Professor Dr Tan Eng Chye and Emeritus Newcastle VC & South Australia's Chief Scientist Dr (Med) Caroline McMillen; and

(c) *Four-Person Research Project Working Team* (RPWT) with Co-Lead Researcher Glasgow Professor Dr Cecilia Tortajada (formerly professor at the LKY-SPP of NUS) in team with Visiting Fulbright Scholar at NTU affiliated with Berkeley, Temple & Fulbright Assistant

Professor Gabriel Kaprielian, Co-Lead University of Zurich's Dean of Evolutionary Medicine Professor Dr (Med) Frank Rühli (former visiting professor at NTU's LKCSM) and a skilled Summa cum Laude Yale-NUS Graduate Reader cum Researcher Marcus Chua to inject unabashed intellectual curiosity. Cecilia and Frank authored two chapters in UC Volume III & IV. To assure consistency and completeness, I serve as the overall Convenor-Researcher.

References

Cornman, John, Eric R. Kingson, and Donna Butts. 1998. "What Is a Social Compact? How Would We Know One If We Saw It? Yes, John, There Is a Social Compact." *Generations: Journal of the American Society on Aging* 22, no. 4: 10–14.

Francis. 2020. *Fratelli Tutti.* October 3, 2020. Accessed November 16, 2020. <http://www.vatican.va/content/francesco/en/encyclicals/documents/papa-francesco_20201003_enciclica-fratelli-tutti.html>

Garrett, Laurie. "China Coronavirus: Tough Realities & Possibility of Global Pandemic." Interview by Jan Jekielek. *American Thought Leaders – The Epoch Times.* February 15, 2020. Video, 72:27. <https://youtu.be/Jcthdee6CXs>

Gibbons, Michael, Camille Limoges, Helga Nowotny, Simon Schwartzman, Peter Scott, and Martin Trow. 1994. *The New Production of Knowledge: The Dynamics of Science and Research in Contemporary Societies.* London: Sage.

Greif, Avner. 1998. "Self-Enforcing Political Systems and Economic Growth: Late Medieval Genoa." In *Analytic Narratives*, edited by Robert H. Bates, Avner Greif, Margaret Levi, Jean-Laurent Rosenthal, and Barry R. Weingast, 23–63. Princeton: Princeton University Press.

International Council for Science. 2017. *A Guide to SDG Interactions: From Science to Implementation.* International Council for Science, Paris. Accessed November 16, 2020. <http://pure.iiasa.ac.at/id/eprint/14591/1/SDGs-Guide-to-Interactions.pdf>

Kagan, Jerome. 2009. *The Three Cultures: Natural Sciences, Social Sciences, and the Humanities in the 21st Century.* Cambridge: Cambridge University Press.

About the Author

Anthony SC Teo is Chevalier of the Order Palmes Académique; Founding Corporatised-NTU Troika, COO Teo with President Su & Provost Andersson; and Emeritus Board Member, HBS Global Alumni Governing Board of Directors, Boston (1987–1990). He also received the NTU Pioneer Educator's Award in 2015.

CHAPTER TWO

A SINGAPORE UNIVERSITY SERVING SOCIETY IN A DISRUPTED WORLD

CHEONG HEE KIAT AND CALVIN M.L. CHAN

Introduction

On 17 March 2017, Singapore saw the establishment of a new publicly-funded university (termed an Autonomous University or AU), viz., the Singapore University of Social Sciences (SUSS). This latest addition to the Singapore university landscape was a result of the re-structuring of SIM University (UniSIM), which had functioned as the only private not-for-profit university in Singapore since 2005. A narrative of the re-structuring is given in an earlier publication (Teo, 2018a). The re-formation of UniSIM into SUSS was not merely a matter of governance and funding under the ambit of the Singapore Ministry of Education (MOE), but perhaps, more significantly, it was a strong affirmation of the unique nature of this university in meaningfully addressing the rising needs of the city-state. These needs are centred on two broad areas, viz., skill-up and lifelong learning of its citizenry and workers, and a holistic focus on social needs of the future as depicted in the new name of the university.

Becoming an Autonomous University with the new name focused on the Social Sciences has instilled greater clarity of purpose and vision on how SUSS can serve the society-at-large in an increasingly disrupted world. This essay serves to articulate these and in so doing, it also presents the model of a university that does not only spotlight on academic excellence in its education and research, but also on being a positive force to advance the well-being of the society.

1. SUSS Today

SUSS is distinct among the six publicly-funded AUs in Singapore. Unlike the other universities which cater mainly to fresh school-leavers or new polytechnic graduates for their full-time undergraduate student intake, SUSS has a larger enrolment of working adults who take the part-time undergraduate programmes covering a broad range of disciplines. Notwithstanding, as an AU, SUSS also admits students for full-time studies like the other AUs, but in a limited number of disciplines. So, while there is a growing cohort of school-leavers joining our full-time undergraduate students (see Table 2.1), the primary source of students for SUSS will remain to be working adults. The predominance of part-time students in its enrolment is in line with SUSS's strategic positioning as the university for lifelong learning. Whether they graduate from one or the other paths, SUSS, being their alma mater and the university for lifelong learning, will continue to cater to the learning needs of its graduates throughout their careers.

Furthermore, appreciating that the learning requirements of working adults goes beyond full-fledged degree programmes, to also include stand-alone modular courses as well as smaller bite-sized courses, SUSS has also established a foothold in the Continuing Education and Training (CET) space, working with employers and professional bodies to cater to the continuing education and lifelong learning needs of their employees and members, respectively. In differentiating our offering with that of typical executive training centres in the market, being a university enables SUSS to recognise some of these courses taken with the university for stacking towards typical degree qualifications such as Bachelor, Master and Doctoral degrees, as well as non-degree qualifications such as Certificates, Graduate Certificates, Graduate Diplomas and Professional Certificates. Some of these non-degree qualifications may also be stacked

Table 2.1. SUSS enrolment through the years

Programmes	Enrolment			
	2017	2018	2019	2020
Part-Time Undergraduate	12,651	12,475	12,184	12,708
Full-Time Undergraduate	1,458	1,968	2,460	2,932
Graduate	460	528	605	755
Total	14,569	14,971	15,249	16,395

towards a degree qualification. Towards this end, SUSS has constructed a comprehensive qualification system to enable learners to move in and out of learning while gathering skills and attestations of skills attainment. Such is the spirit of lifelong learning that SUSS is promoting.

In positioning itself as a university with a special (though not sole) emphasis on teaching, SUSS's focus is on providing applied education that is centred on an outcomes-based curriculum, relevant to professional practices and industry-based, and that which enables students to attain learning outcomes with strong academic support from the university. Thus, almost all our courses and programmes are geared to addressing professional and industry needs, producing graduates who are work-ready. This explains why most of our programmes have a strong element of industry orientation where students are expected to take on industry-sponsored projects or to fulfil certain practicum or industry attachment as part of the curricula. In fact, some of our courses and programmes are developed and offered in partnership with professional bodies, regulatory agencies or key sectoral players. One example is the ISCA-SUSS Business Analytics Certification programme which is jointly curated and offered by the Institute of Singapore Chartered Accountants (ISCA) to support the continuous professional development needs of its members. Another example is the Bachelor of Public Safety and Security (Honours) programme, which is developed in partnership with the Singapore Ministry of Home Affairs to develop talent for the Ministry as well as for the safety and security industry. Many similar partnerships are developed with other organisations across the public, private and social sectors such as the Building and Construction Authority, the Intellectual Property Office of Singapore, the National Council of Social Service, the Singapore Armed Forces, Alibaba Cloud, Huawei, International Chamber of Commerce Academy, Alzheimer's Disease Association and the Islamic Religious Council of Singapore.

On the learning support front, SUSS has systematically put in place a comprehensive learning support system that provides digital learning materials comprising textbooks, accompanying study guides, blended or full-online interactions, all delivered on an anytime-any-place mobile-enabled basis. Aspects of the SUSS learning system have been presented in a previous publication (Teo, 2018a). When COVID-19 struck, it became evident that the years of dedicated effort spent on building our capability in online learning was profitable, fortuitous and enabling in coping with such a black swan event that greatly afflicted peoples and economies globally, including education. As many universities are compelled to switch to online learning during the pandemic, our early investment into this area has enabled a smooth transition, without causing much disruption to teaching and learning, or even to end-of-semester assessments.

Another distinctiveness of SUSS is our focus on providing applied education in the social sciences as well as disciplines that have a strong impact on human and community development. SUSS sees itself as foremost a teaching university as opposed to a research-intensive university. However, it does not mean that SUSS does not conduct research. Rather, our emphasis is on applied research, which is directed at investigating and solving real problems in the industry, society and the world-at-large, with scholarly rigour, ultimately contributing to human and community development. Such an emphasis not only enables the realisation of our vision in serving society, but also allows our research endeavour to correspond and resonate with our position in being an applied education university. Through the years, SUSS has established a research presence in several areas such as financial technology, gerontology, social work and adult learning.

Impetus for a University of Social Sciences

The social sciences involve the systematic and scientific study of human society. Its purpose is to understand how people and groups behave and influence the world around them. As human society grows more complex over time, social science disciplines are no longer confined to specific areas such as anthropology, psychology, economics, sociology and political science. In fact, multi- and interdisciplinary collaborations are increasingly required and necessary to answer multi-faceted social-related questions. For this reason, SUSS, in taking on Social Sciences in its banner, does not restrict itself to a conventional and narrow focus of social science disciplines, but endeavours to bring the social sciences discourse and considerations into all its disciplines. In serving its lifelong learning role which birthed the university, SUSS continues to offer disciplines in many and

Fig. 2.1. SUSS — A university for our city.

varied disciplines in all its Schools, but infuses the curriculum of every programme with social sciences content and activities. At the same time, there is a need for these other disciplines to be brought into social sciences thinking. Therefore given the rapid and widespread digitalisation that is taking place, the need for technology and the efficacious and forward-looking use of technology is addressed in the programmes dealing with such areas as social work, counselling, and human resources management. Ultimately, our students should be exposed to multi- and interdisciplinary learning so as to be able to deal holistically with problems in our world that tend to be increasingly complex.

Here is an example to illustrate the value that can be created in having a multiple disciplinary coverage in a university of social sciences. A team of interdisciplinary faculty in our university came together to conduct a study on the usage and adoption of technology among senior citizens in Singapore. The team comprised faculty from diverse academic domain areas including Anthropology, Gerontology, Human Factors and Information Systems. While the common assumption was that senior citizens were averse to using technology and were less technology-savvy, the study revealed that such an assumption was an inaccurate over-generalisation of the reality in Singapore. The research discovered that there were seniors who were highly adroit with technology and that the determinant of technology usage among senior citizens lay in the socio-economic and cultural (e.g., education and English-proficiency) endowment of these seniors. No doubt, such findings are already useful in informing policy-making to address the digital divide among senior citizens, but this would not have maximised the potential of the inter-disciplinary team. Thus, the team proceeded to develop a set of user interface design guidelines that could be used by developers to design senior-friendly information technology solutions. The guidelines that the team produced have since been adopted as a Singapore Standard.

Just as social science research can contribute to the development of a better world, social science education can help students gain a better understanding of the people, the world and the environment that we are living in. Such an education develops in them a deeper sense of social consciousness. In SUSS, we take it a step further by designing our curricula in a way that nurtures in students a heart that cares for the well-being of society, and a habit of serving society. This is through incorporation of social issues and awareness within the curriculum and involving students in service-learning projects. Students also travel overseas for visits and attachments that open their eyes to the world around them with all its vagaries, inequalities and manifold socio-economic situations. By the time students graduate, they would have developed a "DNA of thinking" that is not only academically rigorous, but also socially aware.

2. Universities and the SDGs

To further illustrate the importance of the social sciences and the impetus for a university of social sciences, reference can be made to the Sustainable Development Goals (SDGs) under the United Nations Development Programme (United Nations, 2015). The first of the 17 SDGs is the eradication of poverty. While most would not usually associate Singaporeans with poverty, a recent study has revealed there are a thousand homeless people sleeping on the streets of Singapore (*Straits Times*, 2019*b*). Although most of these homeless people do not fall under the objective World Bank measure of poverty as someone earning less than US$1.90 a day, they can nonetheless be perceived to be living in poverty within the context of Singapore. Indeed, the picture of poverty and its severity are contextual and relative, depending on local and national definitions and situations. Even in a country like Singapore, poverty has still been regarded as being present (Teo, 2018*b*). Such is the contribution that social science research can make, to understand social disconnects and determine how these may be addressed to alleviate the dire circumstances of the poor.

While each of the goals is important in its own right, they are not standalone in terms of manifestation, outcome or effect on society. Each can strongly relate to other SDGs and are synergistically linked. Some studies have attempted to construe linkages among some of the SDGs — an example is one (Griggs *et al*, 2017) which examines linkages between SDG1: No poverty, SDG2: Zero hunger, SDG3: Good health & well-being, SDG7: Affordable & clean energy and SDG14: Life below water, with the other SDGs. Such studies can inform policy-making, priorities and implementation strategies for optimal benefit and impact.

From the university's perspective, here is another set of linkages that centre on SDG4: Quality education. Eradication of poverty is not the only goal in the list of SDGs that the university can address as it operates within the city. These other goals include SDG4: Quality education, SDG3: Good health & well-being, SDG5: Gender equality, SDG8: Decent work & economic growth, SDG9: Industry innovation & infrastructure, SDG10: Reduced inequalities, and SDG11: Sustainable cities & communities (see Figure 2.2). Central to these may well be Quality of Education which the university can provide, leading to improvements in the other named SDGs. The SDGs mentioned are of particular importance and critical concern in cosmopolitan urban settings, especially inner cities, where many universities are sited. The problem can only grow as urban popula-tions enlarge, placing an even greater challenge, but also an opportunity, for universities to respond effectively in presenting practical solutions and empowering their graduates to contribute to those solutions.

Yet, when one considers Education operating in this relationship with the other SDGs, it is not just *Quality* that is needed — education should be accessible, inclusive, affordable, available and learner-supported and

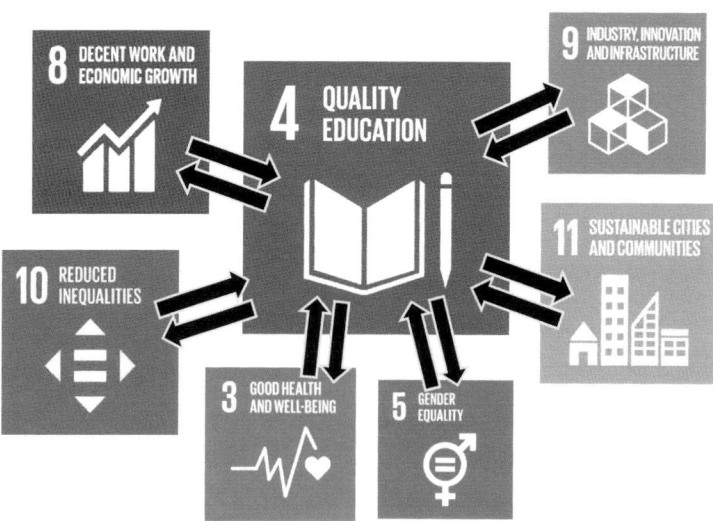

Fig. 2.2. Strong linkage of quality education with other SDGs.

lifelong. A priority is to help the poor financially to obtain an education, so that they can have the chance to level up from their poverty. For what is the use of "quality education" to these poor if they are not able to acquire it? The last condition is also moot, though increasingly recognised, because poverty and wealth are not static conditions in a life span. It is the promotion and provision of continuing lifelong learning that can enhance social mobility and enable uplift of living conditions and sustenance of living standards. A growing concern is what technological and economic changes will render jobs to be lost, permanently, or workers to be dis-located from jobs they can be gainfully employed in. It is not just about entrants to the job market who are disadvantaged by skills mismatch, but also those in mid-career, the PMEs (professionals, managers and executives) in particular, who are not able to transit well into the next job. Post-COVID-19, "online" will likely play a dominant role in many facets of business and life. Online education will be a common mode, perhaps, the main mode in some settings. This will enhance the reach of education, benefitting the poor, but at the same time, if there is a technological gap between the poor and the rest of society, the poor will continue to be disadvantaged. Thus, it is imperative for universities to sense not only the academic needs of learners but also their environment of learning and the means to access online learning.

Universities have a critical and needed role in providing the type and quality of education that will address the above issues. SUSS has been responding to this role, in providing an applied education described in this chapter, helping PMEs and mid-careerists to re-skill for their next jobs, and providing CET education to deepen skills and competencies. At the same time, SUSS is making online education more accessible especially through mobile modes, keeping costs low for an affordable education and raising funds to help those who need assistance financially through their studies. PMEs are experiencing particular vulnerability in Singapore (*Straits Times*, 2019a, *Straits Times*, 2020a) as its economy re-structures amidst global competition and a growing threat to globalisation. More can be done to bring governments, industry, social organisations and the community together to tackle the problems, and the universities can help seed discussions, initiatives and projects towards this end (*Straits Times*, 2020b).

From Social Consciousness to Social Good

The SUSS curriculum goes beyond in-class learning. We believe in educating the whole person in terms of cultivating each one cognitively, socially and creatively through multi-faceted and experiential pedagogy, developing the person to be a purposeful global citizen who provides impactful solutions to society.

As part of our full-time undergraduate degree curriculum, students are expected to take part in community engagement to develop in them a sense of social responsibility and a notion of being able to act and make a meaningful contribution to society. Through such engagement, meaningful connection with the community is harnessed that enhances society's well-being, and also grooms students to become leaders in making a positive difference to their society.

Besides focusing on Singapore, students are also encouraged to explore and engage in community and developmental work in another country. This helps

Fig. 2.3. SUSS team setting off to Lombok, Indonesia, one of several international project destinations in 2019.

Fig. 2.4. Environment: Catching the low tide, both SUSS and Indonesian Teams worked hand in hand to transplant mangrove saplings in Lombok.

them to become global citizens, bringing them perspectives that they would otherwise not have, perspectives that are possibly quite different from what they are familiar or comfortable with. At the same time, the exposure provides the students with the opportunity to hone their international outlook and cross-cultural intelligence through first-hand interaction and direct encounter with organisations and people from the host countries. Rather than sending our students to the developed world or developing countries in faraway regions, SUSS places emphasis on places in ASEAN, China and India (ACI). These countries and the region have a shared culture and history with Singapore, are within a five to seven hour flight time, and crucially, are the future regions of economic growth and linked closely in the socio-politico-economic spheres.

Some of these community engagement initiatives started by our students include the provision of tutoring and mentoring to primary school children from underprivileged backgrounds, equipping the hearing impaired

Fig. 2.5. Education: Students focused on teaching simple everyday English words instead of the usual ABCs. They incorporated games, song and dance daily to engage the children.

Fig. 2.6. Construction: The team helped make concrete for the flooring of an upcoming multi-purpose classroom for a primary school in a project in Laos.

with social media and digital marketing skills which they can then use to expand the business of their social enterprise, and also serving as translators for migrant workers, helping them to file complaints concerning mistreatments or addressing challenges they encounter. As earlier mentioned, overseas exposures (required as a compulsory graduation requirement for our full-time students) add to the colour of such activities.

3. Careers, Living, Lifelong Learning

The future of work and life is becoming increasingly complex, with the useful lifespan of knowledge becoming ever shorter. Ten years ago, not many would have heard of such terms as "Industry Revolution 4.0", "Financial Technology" or "Blockchain". The rate of technology development and its disruption to how work is conducted will require graduates to have the ability to continually learn new skills and knowledge in order to remain relevant in a fast-changing world.

Adding to this is the demographical changes of an ageing population. It is projected that by 2030, one in four Singaporeans will be at least 65 years old (*Straits Times*, 2017). By 2050, the median age of the Singapore workforce is expected to rise to 53.7 years, from 40.6 years in 2010. Many of us will not only be living longer, but will also likely have to remain active in the workforce longer.

Coupling these trends, some have envisioned that the youths of today may have to plan for multiple careers in their lifetime. This will not only result in the need for continuous and lifelong learning, but also requires the capability to effectively navigate the demands of work and life as student life and professional working life will no longer be discreet phases in a person's life-journey, but the two will be interspersed throughout a person's life.

Students in our *part-time* undergraduate programmes and graduate programmes are no strangers to the juggling of identities between being a student and being a working professional as many of them are already doing so. The curriculum and its delivery modes to these learners are precisely designed to enable them to take on work and study concurrently. Upon graduation, these students will be among the most-ready individuals to take on the new future of work and life.

In preparing students in our *full-time* undergraduate programmes for the new future of work and life, learning activities not only imbue students with industry-relevant domain-specific knowledge and skills, but also endow them with a breadth and diversity of knowledge so that they can be sufficiently adept in picking up new knowledge and skills as they traverse through different careers and roles throughout their lifetime.

4. Relevant and Work-Ready

Beyond preparing students who are future-ready, SUSS also invests in developing students who are industry-relevant and work-ready. There are quite a few approaches adopted to ensure this, and a handful are described here.

Unlike most traditional universities, which employ full-time faculty to teach, the bulk of the teaching staff in SUSS are part-time Associate Faculty, many of whom hold full-time professional jobs and have years of rich and relevant professional experience. They often complement our full-time faculty as they bring with them practical knowledge of how the concepts and theories taught in the classroom are applicable in real-life professional contexts. And sometimes, for the students, the practices and the outcomes they encounter in the market help them appreciate and understand better the theories they have to learn in class — a kind of what may be viewed as "reverse-mode" learning. From time to time, prominent guest speakers from the industry are also invited to share with students the latest developments in the fields, and also their personal experiences and reflections.

Besides bringing these practitioners into the classroom, it is acknowledged that nothing quite compares with actually spending time in the trenches of professional life for a first-hand experience. For students who do not possess relevant professional experience, extended practicum or work attachment is often a requirement for graduation. For example, in our Social Work and Counselling programmes, students are required to fulfil hundreds of practicum hours when they are placed with an agency or clinic to practise what they have learned under the guidance and supervision of an experienced professional. Besides attending to clients, students also pick up case management and administration skills as well as learn about the operations of such organisations. Moreover, such practicum or work attachment opportunities are not restricted just to within Singapore. With the growing emphasis on regionalisation of our economy, students may also take on practicum or work attachment in the region, such as the ACI.

SUSS also offers a number of Work-Study programmes, in which after spending one year of full-time study in these degree programmes, students may proceed to take on professional work at an organisation while still continuing their studies in SUSS. An example is the Work-Study Degree that SUSS runs in partnership with the Standard Chartered Bank, where students work for three days a week at the Bank and spend two days studying in SUSS. The Work-Study programme is designed to enable students to gain practical experience of the content knowledge and learning they are presented with on campus. While deepening their appreciation of the application of such knowledge, the Work-Study programme presents the opportunity for students to gain income and seniority in the workplace while completing their studies. Work and training merge at the workplace. The faculty and the workplace supervisor jointly design, supervise and assess the training for the student on site. The nexus with industry needed to make this successful also means that such graduates are more ready and useful to industry when they leave the university. In this way also, those who cannot afford at the outset to pay fully for their university studies can now do so. The university, through this Work-Study opportunity, is thus serving to close the gaps of socio-economic divides, giving opportunities for the poorer sections of the communities to level up.

Adding to this is an effort now by SUSS to recognise prior learning of an individual, particularly that which has been gained from work. This Recognition of Prior Learning (or RPL) enables an individual to have a leg-up in admission into the university, gaining credits towards a qualification. More importantly, it is a tool to affirm what competencies an individual has and at what level, giving him confidence in applying them and moving along a learning path. Within an organisation, such RPL can provide an inventory of the skills and competencies of its employees for planning and deployment.

5. Ingredients for Success

In order to realise SUSS's purpose and vision, the support and partnership of the industry and community are key. Be it opportunities for students to put their social consciousness into action by doing social good, or opportunities for students to carry out practicum, attachment or work-study, SUSS cannot achieve these single-handedly. It is only through partnering industry players and community agencies that we are able to deliver a relevant and holistic education to our students. The result of these will in-turn serve the industry and community as SUSS will then be able to produce work-ready and socially-minded graduates.

Another key ingredient for success is our ability in catering to the needs of our diverse student population, comprising fresh-school leavers as well as working adults. Their needs are different and their expectations vary. Hence, besides the respective academic schools, a number of centres have been established in seeing to their needs. One of these is our Teaching and Learning Centre (TLC) which promotes excellence in teaching and supports the learning needs of our students. Many of the working adults who join our programmes may be anxious about returning to school after a long hiatus from being a student. They need support and encouragement to re-integrate into studying life, while also juggling with work as well as family and social commitments at the same time. The TLC offers various initiatives to support such transition. One of these is to train new students to pick up self-directed learning skills that will serve them well in their transition to become lifelong learners. The Associate Faculty are critical to student success. SUSS pays increasing attention to train and equip these associates, through compulsory courses before deployment, developmental courses to enhance their capabilities once they are in service, and professional courses that can earn them up to a Master degree in Adult Learning.

With SUSS being a flag bearer for adult learning in Singapore, the government has re-structured the Institute for Adult Learning (IAL) to be an autonomous institute within SUSS. The IAL was set up in 2008 to develop and professionalise the adult education sector, conduct research on workforce development and lifelong learning, and drive innovative practices in adult learning. Given the clear synergies between IAL and SUSS in terms of the rich know-how and experience in adult learning and lifelong learning, having IAL within SUSS will catalyse the development of these domains not only in SUSS, but also in Singapore and even internationally.

To provide for the experiential learning of students in terms of community engagement, as well as practicum and attachment, the Centre for Experiential Learning (CEL) was set up in SUSS. The centre looks after the service-learning needs of students, working with students to develop their community engagement projects. CEL also looks after the holistic development of students in terms of cultivating various soft skills such as leadership, teamwork, global competency, cultural awareness and active citizenship. Besides these, the Centre supports the career development of these students by developing work-relevant skills and knowledge and even job-seeking skills.

6. Conclusion

Technology disruption, demographic changes, and more recently the COVID-19 pandemic are all transforming the world that we know. This transformation has extensive ramifications on global economic and social structures, and on employment and livelihoods. These changes have accentuated not only the importance of the social sciences in helping societies to cope, but also the need to have individuals with a sense of responsibility in taking action to do good and making a positive difference.

As has been the focus of this series of Univer-Cities conferences, universities are an important constituent of their cities. They can have impactful and enduring effects upon the development of the cities where they are situated. Ever since its inception as UniSIM in 2005 and subsequent re-structuring as an Autonomous University, SUSS has embraced this notion of being an institutional citizen of our city-state. Becoming an Autonomous University and assuming our new identity as SUSS has heightened this notion and instilled greater clarity of purpose and vision with regard to how SUSS is serving the society-at-large in an increasingly disrupted world. Our approach to applied social science *research* and to applied social science *education* serves to advance the well-being of our society. Our emphasis on lifelong learning and our commitment to being industry-relevant and producing work-ready graduates will address not only the talent development needs of the industry sectors, but also the employment and livelihood of our graduates.

As the world continues to transform, universities will also need to evolve and change in tandem, remaining relevant to their cities. What SUSS has done is adapting to such a need, and in doing so, we maintain the relevance of our university in this city of Singapore.

For more information on SUSS, visit <www://suss.edu.sg>.

References

Griggs, D. J. *et al.*, eds. (2017). "A Guide to SDG Interactions: From Science to Implementation". International Council for Science, Paris, <http://pure.iiasa.ac.at/id/eprint/14591/1/SDGs-Guide-to-Interactions.pdf>

Straits Times Online (6 December 2017). "Singapore's demographic time bomb: Number of old people will match number of young for first time next year, says UOB analyst".

Straits Times (14 June 2019a). "Bulk of retrenched residents in Q1 are PMETs".

Straits Times (9 November 2019b). "1,000 homeless people sleeping on the streets in S'pore: Study".

Straits Times (27 February 2020a). "New job council aims to match retrenched PMEs with vacancies".

Straits Times (23 July 2020b). "New social compact needed in post-COVID-19 world: Tharman".

Teo, Anthony SC, ed. (2018a). *Univer-Cities: Strategic Dilemmas of Medical Origins and Selected Modalities: Water, Quantum Leap & New Models Volume III*. Singapore: World Scientific Publishing Company.

Teo, You Yenn (2018b). *This is What Inequality Looks Like*. Singapore: Ethos Books.

United Nations (2015). "Transforming our World: The 2030 Agenda for Sustainable Development". United Nations Declaration A/RES/70/1.

About the Authors

Cheong Hee Kiat is President of the Singapore University of Social Sciences.

Calvin M.L. Chan is Director, Office of Graduate Studies, Singapore University of Social Sciences.

CHAPTER THREE

PERSPECTIVES FROM THE NATIONAL UNIVERSITY OF SINGAPORE ON COVID-19, BEFORE AND BEYOND

TAN ENG CHYE

When I spoke at the Singapore University of Social Sciences (SUSS) in late 2019, the topic of contention then was how universities could play a role in promoting sustainable development in an era of disruptive change. There was little to no expectation then that the first great disruptive event of the 21st century would soon be upon us, in the form of the COVID-19 global pandemic.

We have watched with distress as the pandemic savaged economies, health systems, and communities across the world. Many lives have been lost, many societies are grieving, and untold millions have been economically displaced. Even with a successful vaccine, the debilitating social and economic effects of the pandemic are likely to linger for years.

In Singapore, the impact of COVID-19 has led the government to draw down an unprecedented S$100 billion, or 20% of the country's GDP, from the nation's carefully husbanded reserves, to shore up the economy, mitigate the most adverse effects, and prepare for a changed global landscape.

As the world continues to grapple with COVID-19, we have begun to assess the pandemic's impact and potential aftermath. In some instances, it has not significantly altered deep-seated forces of structural change whose trajectories were already underway. Indeed, it has accelerated the rate of change, by compressing time frames, and by forcing mass adoption of new norms and technologies. In other dimensions, it has introduced greater uncertainty and fluidity, and individuals, organisations and nations must become more adept in acting with greater agility and flexibility.

For universities, this up-tempo in rate of change will require that we respond with a renewed sense of urgency and inventiveness if we are to play a revitalising role in a human landscape now marked by a deep sense of fragility and anxiety.

In my presentation at SUSS in late 2019, the major disruptive forces I discussed centred around the Fourth Industrial Revolution, and the impact of new technologies on employment and careers, making necessary a lifetime of training and re-skilling. This remains valid, but the changed employment landscape in the aftermath of COVID-19 may require that universities re-examine the scale, depth and duration of our undergraduate and post-graduate training and career support.

The complex ramifications of COVID-19 are still unfolding. However, the need for planning and swift action in a changed environment lies in our immediate present. A good starting point would be to examine key global trends that have emerged in the COVID-19 environment, before considering how universities can contribute positively to recovery, locally and globally.

A World in Flux

Pre-COVID 19, the Asian Development Bank (ADB) had projected that by 2050, Asia's share of global GDP would reach 52% by 2050, and the region's per capita income in purchasing power parity (PPP) terms would increase six-fold to reach present-day European levels.[1] Asia would once again become the centre of the world's economic engine, a position it had not held since before the era of European colonialism.

It is difficult to accurately ascertain the damage or possible reversals that COVID-19 has done to these projections: Asia is vast and heterogenous, with nations at differing levels of development and capabilities. Early indications are that the more developed countries of East Asia — Japan, South Korea and China — have emerged with their economic capabilities relatively intact, and are working resolutely towards recovery and growth.

This does not mean a straight-forward resumption of status quo. There has been speculation that companies may move away from their hitherto "China-plus-one strategy",[2] in favour of diversifying their supply chain and logistics to more locations outside China, with greater emphasis on resilience and redundancies. Such a change might present opportunities for Southeast Asia.

Another speculation suggests that with recovery in Europe and the US expected to lag, intra-Asian trade flows would be best poised to recover and grow, furthering the integration and linkages within Asia that has been taking place. In 2019, a McKinsey report had estimated that "60 percent of goods traded by Asian economies are within the region, 71 percent of Asian investment in start-ups and 59 percent of foreign direct investment (FDI) is intraregional, and 74 percent of Asian travel(l)ers travel within the region".[3]

These two scenarios might seem positive and reassuring for Asia, but much is contingent on the pivotal, and often uneasy relationship between the world's two largest economies — China and the US. Writing for the July/August 2020 issue of *Foreign Affairs*, Singapore's Prime Minister, Mr Lee Hsien Loong, noted that both nations have to find a new equilibrium in their relationship, a "modus vivendi" that allows for healthy competition and reduces the possibility of confrontation and conflict.[4] Otherwise, continuing tensions could see a rise in global and regional instability, with negative consequences for many countries, particularly in Asia. In a sobering assessment, Mr Lee observed that the oft-touted Asian century is "neither inevitable nor foreordained".

Digitalisation Accelerated

Microsoft CEO Satya Nadella expressed that COVID-19 had compressed "2 years' worth of digital transformation in two months". Digitalisation, and its impact on work and employment, might prove to be one of the most far-reaching effects wrought by the pandemic.

Working-from-home (WFH) became the norm all across the world during the height of the pandemic. One estimate had 50% of the US workforce in WFH mode;[5] in Singapore, the figure has been as high as 80%.

But the economic impact of WFH extends far beyond work culture and routines. If the future of work now necessarily includes the home, demand for office space might fall, or be in need of radical re-design. This carries broad implications for the construction sector, as well as transportation- and infrastructure-related industries.

During this prolonged, enforced stay-home period, one category of enterprises that benefitted was e-commerce. Reports suggested that curbside pickup in the US surged 208% between 1 and 20 April, and online sales jumped 49% from 12 March to 11 April.[6] Amazon hired an additional 100,000 workers in the US to cope with the increased volume, with another 50,000 temporary hires in India.[7] Shopee, a leading e-commerce platform in Asia, reported the total number of orders at 429.8 million for the first quarter, compared to 203.5 million for the same period the previous year.[8]

E-commerce requires seamless transactional experiences, tightly integrated logistics, robust data security, and intelligent demand sensing. As online commerce becomes an increasing norm, we should anticipate rapid and sustained innovation in areas such as cloud computing, data analytics, A.I., robotics, and "last-mile" delivery solutions, such as drones. Those with in-demand skills and expertise can expect an advantageous employment market.

On a broader level, WFH would seem to benefit both employees and employers, offering reduced overheads and increased flexibility. There could be a pronounced shift to hybrid workforces, comprised of a fluid blend of onsite and remote nodes. However, there is one important caveat we should be mindful of: free of geographic boundaries, workers may find themselves competing globally for the best opportunities.[9]

To thrive, workers will have to be "multimodal", adapting fluidly to new situations, integrating seamlessly with global teams, and contributing uniquely by drawing on a broad array of skills and experience, which are constantly refreshed through training.

E-learning also became the default mode during this pandemic. Schools at every level closed, and learning became virtual. Results have varied,[10] and consensus opinion would be that virtual learning cannot yet replace the classroom. Nonetheless, the pandemic might have significantly accelerated the integration of digital and physical learning environments.

During this period at NUS, all lectures with more than 50 students went online, as did a few of our exam modules. We are currently collating data and results, but we expect to introduce and integrate more e-learning elements, even after the pandemic has passed.

The growing acceptance of e-learning as a delivery mode has important implications for the higher education sector. Lower barriers to competition could see aggressive new players such as Massive Open Online

Courses (MOOCs) seeking a larger local and global market share. On the flip side, universities that may have refrained from international campuses due to costs and risks, might explore setting up an e-learning channel at relatively lower cost, widening the pool of potential students.

In theory, e-learning is the platform most suited to the demands of continuous adult learning, in terms of offering scale, access, customisation and constant adaptability. It will be powerfully supported by analytics, to derive the battery of metrics that will track, likely in real-time, student progress, learning outcomes, and teaching effectiveness.[11] More accurate tracking could in-turn allow for a more precisely calibrated credential system, signalling the alignment between learner capabilities and industry needs.

Sustainable Communities, Sustainable Development

One of the more disquieting themes that has emerged from this pandemic was the issue of access to healthcare, with the poor, the vulnerable and the marginalised fearful that they would not be prioritised in event of infection.

The sharp economic downturn also led to waves of layoffs and a consequent surge in unemployment. Although many sectors of the global economy were hard-hit, a McKinsey report on the virus' impact on the European job market estimated that "80 percent of jobs at risk (46 million) are held by people who do not hold a tertiary degree", and those without a university degree are twice at risk of job loss as those with tertiary education.[12] A second McKinsey report, this time on the US job market, echoed broadly the same findings, saying that one-third of US jobs were at risk, with more than 80% of those held by low-income workers.[13]

The protracted issue of inequality and social economic divide, in both developed and developing nations, is not new. But the disproportionate impact on COVID-19 on those members of society least able to absorb disruption or dislocation has brought these long-standing tensions to the fore, highlighting the frayed social compact in many developed countries, and for certain developing nations, the relative absence of social safety nets.

Events such as COVID-10 then become a potential flash point that can trigger widespread social unrest. In extreme cases, such protests escalate to become systemic risks, jeopardising order and stability, and further eroding social bonds and trust.

When COVID-19 passes, the world will be much changed. Familiar jobs would have disappeared, and new ones, requiring new skills, will take their place. Workers will need extensive support and training investment as they retrain and adapt. Industries will have to adjust to radically different conditions.

Institutions of Higher Learning (IHLs) such as universities have an opportunity to play a powerful catalytic and transformative role. They can prepare new generations of young people for a very different economic future, and offer an integrated lifelong learning programme that provides workers with a continual opportunity to acquire new skills and capabilities. In tandem, educational institutions will also have to guide learners on the development of traits such as resilience, adaptability and curiosity.

Discussions revolving around sustainability have often centred on mitigating climate change through concerted action, reduced consumption, and breakthrough innovation, such as clean sources of energy. The United Nation's Sustainable Development Goals Agenda, as well as the Paris Agreement, both envision broad change driven by all sectors of society, encompassing objectives such as reducing inequality and encouraging economic growth for wider prosperity.

Nevertheless, to make bold and inspired choices about the future, societies need to feel confident, vibrant and cohesive. If, instead, they are fractious and anxious, it will be difficult to summon the broad support needed for structural change, which often requires a present sacrifice for future gain. In addition, tackling deep-seated social challenges often requires new resources and capabilities that only economic growth can generate.

Sustainable communities and sustainable development are not contradictory terms. Rather, they are mutually reinforcing, synergistically creating a brighter and more hopeful future.

Singapore: Impacted, but Moving Ahead

As an open global economy heavily dependent on trade flows, Singapore has been severely impacted by COVID-19. Present estimates are that

GDP will decline by between 4 and 7% for 2020. Our Prime Minister has described the pandemic as "the crisis of a generation".

In the nation's recovery plans, the underlying premise is that a vibrant society is essentially inseparable from a strong economy. Singapore sought, firstly, to alleviate the most severe immediate effects on businesses and individuals, and to protect livelihoods; secondly, to mobilise society, and commit resources, for a very different future.

A comprehensive suite of programmes and initiatives was introduced, aimed at raising the resilience and dynamism of both the workforce and companies. For companies, the focus was on digital transformation, to meet increased competition; for workers, to prepare for a future where new skills and new ways of working will be required.

As of early June 2020, Singapore had exited its "circuit breaker", or lockdown phase, although many social and business activities remained restricted, including retail and F&B. The number of COVID-19 cases has been largely contained, with limited community transmission. Although the number of cases among our migrant workers community has climbed, due to spread within dormitories and places of interaction, the vast majority of cases have mild symptoms. Overall fatality rates have remained low.

Singapore's preparedness to deal with pandemics was the result of painful lessons learnt during the outbreak of Severe Acute Respiratory Syndrome (SARS) in 2003. Since then, Singapore has invested significantly in upgrading our ability to deal with infectious diseases, including the building of the National Centre for Infectious Diseases (NCID), a 330-bed purpose-built facility for treatment and prevention. Fortuitously, it officially opened in September 2019.

Singapore also took the unusual step during the pandemic of assuring the leaders of foreign nations that their migrant workers with COVID-19 will be extended the fullest range of care possible, including protection of wages, medical treatment, food and lodging, without charge. This was an affirmation of our duty of care, as well as recognition of the many contributions migrant workers have made to our community and economy.

Post COVID-19, there will be a major drive to digitalise the business operations of our 270,000 small and medium-sized enterprises (SMEs) that account for 72% of our total employment. Through digitalisation, our SME's will become more nimble, more efficient, and more resilient and adaptable to changes in their industry or global environment.

The other priority centres on jobs and employment. New jobs will require new sources of growth, and companies will also need a period of adjustment. Post-pandemic, some jobs will not return, and workers will have to reskill and retrain for new positions. Singapore's unique solution is the "tripartite" arrangement, where the government works in close concert with businesses and unions to identify, re-position and match jobs in the changed economy.

The centrepiece of this effort is the National Jobs Council, which will include eight government ministers, as well as leaders of unions and business associations. The target will be to support 100,000 job seekers over the immediate 12-month period through creating new vacancies, traineeships and skills training places. This includes 40,000 jobs, 25,000 traineeships and 30,000 skills training opportunities. Special attention and assistance will be given to older workers who are more vulnerable to displacement, and need more support.

This national emphasis on retraining and skills upgrading has been ongoing for a few years. Known as the SkillsFuture initiative, it seeks to establish lifelong learning as a national movement and a key plank of our competitiveness. A comprehensive framework has been adopted, covering industry requirements, benchmarking qualifications, and creating upgrading pathways for workers. Over time, retraining has become more widely accepted by both workers and companies. In 2019, some 500,000 individuals and 14,000 enterprises benefitted from SkillsFuture.

There are some promising indicators that Singapore's established reputation as a fast-moving, forward-looking city continues to help us stand out against the competition. The Economic Development Board (EDB) reported that in the first quarter of 2020, we secured S$13 billion of investment commitments, against an original target of S$8-$10 billion for the whole year.[14]

NUS: An Integrated and Synergistic University, Deeply Aligned with National Goals

In the immediate period following the onset of COVID-19, the focus of the National University of Singapore (NUS) was on the safety and well-being of our community. Like many other universities, we introduced a range of measures, including physical distancing, virtual learning and contact tracing protocols.

We then turned our attention to mid-term issues arising from the pandemic's impact, particularly on our graduating cohort. The key concern was the downturn in the employment market. In 2019, more than 90% of our cohort secured jobs within six months after graduation; the situation in 2020 is likely to be much more challenging.

In response, we launched the NUS Resilience and Growth Initiative 2020, with the aim of helping our graduating cohort locate job openings, assisting qualifying in-campus students with enhanced financial aid, and reinforcing a sense of community through start-up projects that benefit society.

We aim to provide 200 jobs within NUS to our new alumni, with another 800 apprenticeship positions with partner enterprises. In addition, we wanted to kick-start their lifelong learning journey, so we are offering four continuing education modules free to recent graduates, which they can select from a catalogue of 150 modular and short courses.

Programmes such as job-matching and financial aid target the individual student. But we also wanted to emphasise our support for the wider community, and offer our graduates an opportunity to give back. Therefore, we launched the unique "Make X Better" Innovation Challenge, with 'X' standing for People, Society and the World. The initiative encourages small start-up teams to explore ideas and projects that positively impact society. These themes include ensuring mental wellness, improving food security, and tackling climate change. Participating teams will receive stipends and project funding for a specific duration.

Pre-COVID 19, NUS had been extensively considering for some time how the institution, and our students, can best adapt and thrive in a fast-changing world. The magnitude of the changes taking place around us led us to conclude that we had to make bold shifts, not just incremental adjustments.

There were two major trends identified: first, the changing nature of work, and how best to prepare our future graduates not only for greater opportunity, but also greater uncertainty; the second was the need to raise the impact of universities, with particular reference to tackling complex challenges that often require a holistic and integrated approach.

NUS's endeavours are centred around three main pillars: education, research, and innovation and enterprise.

Education

For several decades now, the focus of universities was on pre-employment training (PET). This was appropriate when graduates entering the workforce could expect "a career for a lifetime". Now, the model has been flipped on its head: graduates should expect a "lifetime of careers", with shorter tenures between jobs, and a limited shelf life for skills and knowledge.

In this dynamic environment, lifelong learning is the strongest hedge we can offer to ensure life-time employability. Learning has to be both continuous and career-spanning, with new skills constantly being picked up and synthesised. Continuing Education and Training (CET) has to be integrated as part of a wider framework that links self-development and employment opportunities.

For our students to be "future-ready", undergraduate education has first to be remodelled. Students are no longer passive receptables of content, but rather active agents, and the emphasis has shifted towards flexibility, interactivity and experiential learning. Alongside deep domain expertise, students also require horizontal competencies, to develop intellectual versatility and to prepare them for a lifetime of continuous learning.

We introduced a General Education (GE) framework that offers a broad range of topics distinctively separate from each student's disciplinary interest. The General Education framework has two layers: at one layer, we offer basic courses from the Humanities, Social Sciences and Sciences, to familiarise students with the modes of thinking in these disciplines, to think critically in these domains and to broaden their perspectives. We then offer a second layer of interdisciplinary courses that expose students to cross-disciplinary thinking and skills. At present, students take five GE modules, but we are aiming to increase this to ten GE modules eventually.

The intention is to develop higher-order qualities of the mind, a capacity to think both critically and creatively, within and across disciplines, and to nurture an intellectual literacy which will form the foundation of their lifelong learning journey, which may well last 40 to 50 years.

We further reinforced this push towards intellectual breath by offering some 180 combinations of Double Major and Major-Minor degree programmes, and aim to have 50% of each cohort trained in more than one discipline within the next five years. Another learning innovation was the grade-free year for our freshmen, to encourage exploration of topics outside their field of study.

On lifelong learning, we launched the NUS Lifelong Learners or NUS L³ programme, a paradigm-shifting initiative wherein every NUS student enrolment will be valid for 20 years from point of undergraduate admission. This allows our 300,000 alumni to access a wide range of courses, ranging from short modules to full post-graduate programmes. These courses are nationally certified and emphasise skills-based learning and industry relevance.

Besides L³, we also offer the CET 500 programme for the wider public and enterprises. This programme allows for selection and customisation of our entire range of CET courses to meet specific industry and company needs.

Adult learning offers great potential for innovation and new approaches. Exciting lines of development include pedagogical improvement, as well as integrating technology for maximum learning impact and efficiency. To strengthen our expertise in CET and to co-ordinate our efforts on a campus-wide basis, we established the Institute for Application of Learning Science and Educational Technology (ALSET), and the School of Continuing and Lifelong Education (SCALE) respectively.

Research

As Singapore became a more advanced economy, R&D took on an increasingly important role in sharpening our competitive edge and in driving innovation. The Research, Innovation and Enterprise (RIE) 2020 plan, the centrepiece of our national R&D efforts, has seen the commitment of SGD $19 billion for the period 2016-2020. In 2019, the Ministry of Trade and Industry published a report suggesting that from 2002 to

2017, a 1% increase in R&D stock in a firm led to a 0.135% increase in productivity on average.[15] During this COVID-19 period, the government announced that research funding and support would be maintained.

There have been some positive dividends from our heavy R&D investment. Duke-NUS Medical School was among the first in the world to isolate the SARS-CoV-2 coronavirus that causes COVID-19. A team of NUS multi-disciplinary researchers leveraged on artificial intelligence to work out the optimal dosage of drugs that can be used in combination for the treatment of Covid-19 patients. Tychan, a biotech company, which is co-founded by Professor Ooi Eng Eong, also from Duke-NUS, is about to start a Phase 1 clinical safety trial for an antibody drug for the virus.[16]

Some years ago, when NUS surveyed the research landscape and considered how we could deepen our research capabilities, and raise our impact, we concluded that our strongest option would be integrated, multi-disciplinary clusters, because the most promising breakthroughs happen at the intersection of two or more disciplines.

Furthermore, to address some of the world's complex challenges, solutions would need to encompass technological, scientific and societal aspects. This multi-disciplinary approach plays to our broad-based research strengths and the advancement of holistic and comprehensive solutions. We were also mindful that the commitment of the nation's resources in research had to deliver community benefit and support national advancement.

We have since identified eight different themes with both an Asian and Singapore relevance: Ageing, Asian Studies, Biomedical Science and Translational Medicine, Finance & Risk Management, Integrative Sustainability Solutions, Maritime, Material Science, and Smart Nation.

Smart Nation represents one of our most promising clusters. Its aim is to harness the latest physical and digital technologies, integrate them seamlessly into our living environment and support a dynamic and diverse economy which offers opportunities for all. i4.0, a dedicated facility, is the focal point of our digital innovation efforts, grouping together our inter-disciplinary research entities, such as artificial intelligence, data science, analytics, modelling, simulation and optimisation, and cybersecurity. To drive greater synergy, i4.0 also brings together entrepreneurs and VCs, to build a complete ecosystem and value chain that spans idea to marketplace.

Another key research cluster is the Integrative Sustainability Solutions cluster that explores issues such as clean energy materials and systems, environmental surveillance and treatment of urban waterways, waste-to-energy conversion, seawater desalination and sustainable urban transport systems, within a tropical, urban and Asian context.

Understandably, COVID-19 has dominated media coverage and public attention over the last few months. But we should not be distracted from undertaking research, and pursuing innovation on other equally important issues looming on the horizon. Otherwise, the consequences for nations and communities could be severe.

Foremost among these issues would be climate change. As a small, low-lying island nation, rising sea waters represent an existential threat to Singapore's existence. Given the scale of scientific and technical challenges, the government has estimated that securing Singapore against rising sea levels may cost SGD $100 billion over 100 years. To support such a level of expenditure, the government is exploring a series of options, including diversified funding and drawing from our reserves.

Other issues address specific vulnerabilities, such as food security and energy.

Food security became a strategic issue during this COVID-19 period, as trading and shipping schedules were affected. Singapore had earlier announced its aim to increase its food supply resilience by meeting 30% of total food needs by 2030, or a "30 by 30" strategy. Ideas include indoor multi-storey LED lighting for vegetable farms and recirculating aquaculture systems.

Energy security is another long-term effort for Singapore. Currently, 95% of Singapore's electricity is generated using the cleanest form of fossil fuel, natural gas. Solar holds promise, but challenges include its relative level of efficiency and the high incidence of overcast skies in Singapore. By 2030, we aim to have solar power generating 2 gigawatt-peak (GWp), or about 4% of total demand at present levels. Other options under study include regional power grids, and carbon capture utilisation and storage technologies.

No doubt COVID-19 has had an impact on research schedules and outputs. Labs were closed and staff were forced to stay home. In the near term, deliverables will have to be adjusted and funding arrangements may need to be reconsidered, together with grantors and stakeholders.

Going forward, the funding landscape may evolve with tighter budgets and a greater emphasis on outcomes that include a clear or tangible benefit within specific timeframes. Universities may have to carefully balance between supporting society's present needs, while continuing longer-term research necessary to yield the deep insights that underpin quantum leaps in technology and possibilities.

Innovation and Enterprise

Innovation and enterprise (I&E), which includes entrepreneurial education, has become another distinctive trademark of NUS. Innovation and entrepreneurship are essential elements as an economy advances, helping to maximise talent and resources, while securing a higher foothold on the economic value chain.

For some years, we have steadily built up our I&E nodes and networks, both locally and globally. In education, our globally recognised NUS Overseas Colleges (NOCs), embed aspiring students in entrepreneurial hotspots throughout the world, while attending courses at prestigious partner universities. To build and support a pipeline of enterprises, we have Block 71, an ecosystem builder and global connector, usually partnering with established corporations and government agencies across the world. *The Economist* had described Singapore's Block 71 node as "the world's most tightly packed entrepreneurial ecosystem".

For postgraduate members of our community, we have the Graduate Research Innovation Program (GRIP). GRIP is uniquely focused on deep-tech start-ups, offering a comprehensive package that includes industry linkage, mentorship, funding and other necessary support to take postgraduate students and researchers from ideas to marketplace.

More recently, we have turned our focus to Asia, and in particular, Southeast Asia, the region we are most familiar with. The region's rapid economic growth and vast potential offer unrivalled opportunities for transformation and impact through I&E. We have established Block 71 nodes in Jakarta, Bandung, Ho Chi Minh and Suzhou, and NOC programmes in Shenzhen and Yogyakarta.

COVID 19 has necessarily curtailed travel and face-to-face engagements. This will inevitably slow the pace of exchanges and development of ideas and enterprises. For the time being, we have adopted alternative measures such as staggered personnel movement, virtual meetings, and local apprenticeship programmes in place of overseas exchanges and immersion.

In a region fast transforming, innovation and entrepreneurship continue to offer compelling value. The mode of creation may start to alter, post-pandemic, and we will adjust as needed. The direct and hoped-for benefit of I&E are ideas and enterprises that break the mould, and create exciting new value. But an equally important indirect benefit is the mindset of collaboration and cooperation that widespread networks and nodes encourage. At a time when parts of the world are at risk of turning inward and reactionary, such nodes and networks are a powerful demonstration of the value of sharing and cooperation.

Adjusting to New Realities, while Retaining Long-Term Focus

COVID-19 has upended assumptions of routine and normal operating parameters, and forced a series of rapid adjustments across nations, communities, institutions and individuals. As we begin to emerge from its impact, recovery across the world is likely to be tentative and cautious. Properly balanced, universities can play an important role, both in supporting near-term recovery, and in remaining engaged in longer-term priorities that enable broad advancement.

As Singapore's flagship university, our commitment remains steadfast — to raise the well-being of the community through learning, knowledge and innovation, and to expand opportunity for all, so that every member of society can contribute positively and participate fully.

Notes

1. Asian Development Bank, "Asia 2050: Realizing the Asian Century", Executive Summary <https://www.adb.org/sites/default/files/publication/28608/asia2050-executive-summary.pdf>

2. Bill Mongelluzzo, "COVID-19 changes big ship, Asia focus for US ports", 22 April 2020 <https://www.joc.com/maritime-news/trade-lanes/covid-19-changes-big-ship-asia-focus-us-ports_20200422.html>

3. Oliver Tonby et al. "The Future of Asia: Asian flows and networks are defining the next phase of globalization", 18 September 2019 <https://www.mckinsey.com/featured-insights/asia-pacific/the-future-of-asia-asian-flows-and-networks-are-defining-the-next-phase-of-globalization>

4. Lee Hsien Loong, "The Endangered Asian Century: America, China, and the Perils of Confrontation", *Foreign Affairs*, July/August 2020 <https://www.foreignaffairs.com/articles/asia/2020-06-04/lee-hsien-loong-endangered-asian-century?fbclid=IwAR3RKBQ3UPJFurdCwXcjPyd52JUM1IF12fmAnIrUGolvpHU-CabbcD8Ter8>

5. Brian Eastwood, "What happens to industry and employment after COVID-19?", 1 June 2020 <https://mitsloan.mit.edu/ideas-made-to-matter/what-happens-to-industry-and-employment-after-covid-19>

6. Lauren Thomas, "Curbside pickup at retail stores surges 208% during coronavirus pandemic", 27 April 2020 <https://www.cnbc.com/2020/04/27/coronavirus-curbside-pickup-at-retail-stores-surges-208percent.html>

7. Xinhua, "Amazon to hire 50,000 temporary workers in India to cater to surge in online shopping amid COVID-19", 23 May 2020 <http://www.xinhuanet.com/english/2020-05/23/c_139081885.htm>

8. Dylan Loh, "Coronavirus pandemic fuels Asia e-commerce boom", 31 May 2020 <https://asia.nikkei.com/Business/Retail/Coronavirus-pandemic-fuels-Asia-e-commerce-boom>

9. Channel NewsAsia, "Soon you may be competing with talent globally. The Fortitude Budget is a wake-up call", 2 June 2020 <https://www.channelnewsasia.com/news/commentary/remote-working-global-talent-fortitude-budget-skills-singapore--12791642>

10. Cathy Li and Farah Lalani, "The COVID-19 pandemic has changed education forever. This is how". World Economic Forum, 29 April 2020 <https://www.weforum.org/agenda/2020/04/coronavirus-education-global-covid19-online-digital-learning/>

11. Larry Dignan, "Online learning gets its moment due to COVID-19 pandemic", 22 March 2020 <https://www.zdnet.com/article/online-learning-gets-its-moment-due-to-covid-19-pandemic-heres-how-education-will-change/>

12. David Chinn et al., "Safeguarding Europe's livelihoods: Mitigating the employment impact of COVID-19", 19 April 2020 <https://www.mckinsey.com/industries/public-sector/our-insights/safeguarding-europes-livelihoods-mitigating-the-employment-impact-of-covid-19>

13. Susan Lund et al., "Lives and livelihoods: Assessing the near-term impact of COVID-19 on US workers", 2 April 2020 <https://www.mckinsey.com/industries/public-sector/our-insights/lives-and-livelihoods-assessing-the-near-term-impact-of-covid-19-on-us-workers>

14. Zhaki Abdullah, "Singapore secured about S$13 billion in investment commitments in first 4 months of 2020 amid COVID-19 outbreak", 30 May 2020 <https://www.channelnewsasia.com/news/singapore/covid-19-edb-singapore-investments-coronavirus-surpass-projected-12786876>

15. Marsha Teo et al., "Returns to research and development (R&D) among firms in Singapore" <https://www.mti.gov.sg/-/media/MTI/Resources/Economic-Survey-of-Singapore/2019/Economic-Survey-of-Singapore-Third-Quarter-2019/FA_3Q19.pdf>

16. Wing Pei Ting, "Singapore to begin first human trial for potential Covid-19 treatment", *Today Online* Singapore, 10 June 2020 <https://www.todayonline.com/singapore/singapore-begin-first-human-trial-next-week-potential-covid-19-treatment>

About the Author

Tan Eng Chye is President of the National University of Singapore.

CHAPTER FOUR

UNIVER-CITIES PROJECT 2016-2019 UPDATE & CONTINUITY

GORDON JOHNSON

The Univer-Cities project was conceived a decade ago by Anthony Teo Soon Chye, now an Adjunct Professor at Singapore University of Social Sciences. Professor Teo's background, following study at Harvard, was in business and entrepreneurship, and subsequently to addressing challenges in higher education. He served as Secretary to the Nanyang Technological University (NTU) during that institution's period of rapid and innovative growth. Nanyang University as it was known in 1955, from the 1980s formed the technical and vocational component of Singapore's National University. It linked up with the National Institute of Education in 1991 and became a fully autonomous university in 2006. NTU greatly expanded its areas of teaching and research (including the development of humanities, social sciences, and a medical school), and it underwent a major building programme taking its campus beyond its historic home — the delightful Yunnan Garden in the Jurong district of Singapore.

The university's physical expansion had been greatly aided by the decision, in 2008, to locate the 2010 Youth Olympic Games Village at NTU — a project for which Professor Teo chaired the steering committee. During that same period, he was a Visiting Fellow at Wolfson College, Cambridge. Cambridge was also a university that, while boasting a tradition of scholarship reaching back into the thirteenth century, was undergoing a massive expansion and change of mission, especially research in the sciences and bio-medical disciplines. The University could no longer be confined within the boundaries of a relatively small medieval market town.

Until almost the mid-twentieth century, Cambridge, with its nearly unique decentralised organisation and governance, had been predominantly a species of liberal arts college educating mainly young men for positions in church and state. However, a growing volume of distinguished research, rooted in changes in the academic professions begun in the nineteenth century, was much accelerated in the twentieth under the combined pressures of growing general literacy, the development of the professions and new outlets for educated labour, and the advance of scientific research. During that century Cambridge came to be primarily regarded as a major, and particularly diverse, research university of international renown. The increasing demands made of research, and management of the resources needed to make it possible, required different forms of organisation from that of the diffuse Collegiate University at its heart. The physical needs of a greatly increased population of scholars and students, and space for them to work in, outstripped what had been provided previously as part of the town and in the separate independent Colleges. The disciplines, in science and arts alike, required new lecture and seminar rooms, laboratories, libraries, museums, gardens, galleries and farms. The change of scale could not be contained within the boundaries of medieval Cambridge. At the same time, necessity demanded some form of over-arching management, planning and control, but one that would require a light touch if it were not to stifle the creative scholarly anarchy that was a hallmark of the place. As funding for the university's work, particularly but not only in the scientific and technological areas, drew more and more on a diversity of public support, charitable and business partnerships, more formal constitutional and administrative structures evolved, responding to the challenge to make binding decisions in a timely and coherent fashion, and to demonstrate social and political accountability for the resources supplied.

As originally conceived, the Univer-Cities project looked at ways of understanding a number of distinct but interwoven concerns. One was the growing realisation that forms of higher and vocational education could no longer be regarded as completed by conventional three- or four-year undergraduate courses taken by students in their late 'teens and early twenties. The realities of modern life pointed to regular and frequent updating of skills, and of the advantages of continuing professional development. Some sort of formal provision, therefore, must be worked out for what was termed "life-long education", typically requiring short bursts of study tailored to particular purposes. Some of this was simply a matter of learning new skills and techniques, functions which had not conventionally rested with universities and which consequently were perceived as being difficult for incorporating into a university system that was seen by some to have become too distinctly "academic" in purpose.

The twentieth century, with its massive social changes and the profound impact of major wars and unprecedented governmental activity to provide public services, had driven research imperatives located in universities. This had not been their prime purpose, nor was it ever their exclusive purpose, but it propelled institutional developments along new lines. This creative function — to search for new knowledge and better understanding — was itself a massive and complex business. Research had a necessary but ambiguous relationship with social and economic need, and with teaching; it also progressed by a mixture of competition and collaboration. It grew out of established disciplinary interests, but thrived best, and was often at its most disruptive, if there was openness to intermingling of intellectual enquiry and the prospects of working in interdisciplinary ways. It was expensive so had to have institutional frameworks that were both secure and flexible. Further, as the state became increasingly a major player in university affairs, and as a whole splay of economic, social and political interests gathered to draw upon university expertise at all sorts of levels, the notion of universities standing apart from, and operating wholly independently of, the societies to which they belonged became more and more unreal. They had never, in fact, been the isolated "ivory tower" of common perception, even though much controversy would centre round notions of their unresponsiveness to "real life" in competition with arguments from within academia of the case for "academic freedom" to determine what to teach and what to explore.

These and adjacent themes have been explored in a collaborative way between several universities and disciplines over the course of the previous three volumes of conference papers in this Univer-Cities series of books. At the core have been the experiences of Singapore, Cambridge, Berkeley, Hong Kong, Malaysia, Canada, Australia and others — all of which, in different ways, have performed exceptional service to their cities, nations, regions and internationally. What has emerged is the degree to which enhanced co-operation between universities on a global scale is already taking place, though not perhaps adequately recognised as such.

Similarly, the extent to which universities have integrated research into their regular undergraduate teaching programmes, and an actual willingness to devise and run post-first-degree courses for professional development has sometimes been inadequately perceived. This arises partly from the accelerated rate of change and demand, so institutions (and for polemical purposes especially those with long-standing intellectual traditions or having generous provision of endowment income) are criticised for not moving fast enough to stay ahead of the game. Partly also, of course, the ferocity of argument draws strength from the competition for resources — material and human — within and beyond institutions. Applications for more funding bring out the competitive rather than the co-operative side of university work. This applies equally strongly within institutions where each school, faculty, or department feels it has to fight its corner for management time and for the "fair" allocation of support.

Even here, though, in debate the negative aspects of behaviour often triumph over a more positive reality. The most promising theme to emerge so far from the Univer-Cities project has been the extent to which problems of this nature are increasingly being recognised and efforts made to redress them. That universities should work consciously with each other and with external partners is surprisingly common — most clearly seen, for example, in Cambridge's newest science campus to the west of the city (bigger than the whole of the historic city centre) and the bio-medical campus to the south. On these sites, university departments sit alongside spaces occupied by bodies who will go on to apply the fruits of research in commercial and business ways. The bio-medical campus, the largest in Europe, is home to a major hospital, university departments, independent research laboratories funded from both the private sector and from international charities. New building in both Hong Kong and Berkeley, following a pattern used at NTU, has sought deliberately to allow the use of expensive university facilities for community educational and recreational purposes, as well as helping to ameliorate rather than exacerbate the housing and transport problems that have emerged with the growth of cities and consequent overspill of urban populations.

Most promising of all is a slow but steady growing awareness that discovery and application, learning and implementation, hang together in more complex ways than those operating from within particular components would once have acknowledged. The pure science and the innovative scholarship are not sufficient in themselves to create better and more fulfilling lives for all. Indeed, a major challenge remains how unequally knowledge is made easily accessible, and how the benefits it brings are distributed. Indeed, each step forward seems to lead to the establishment of new privileged classes who benefit quickly and exclusively from a technological or medical advance. Access to knowledge, however potentially democratised by technical innovation, has yet to overcome extraordinarily persistent and powerful economic and social barriers. Simple and "inexpensive" digital techniques of learning and research are of no use if teachers don't properly know how to work with them, and if pupils do not have the essential complementary equipment to make connections, or social circumstances that permit them the time to participate. It's actually not straightforward, even in wealthy countries, to equip each child with a suitable computer. The pattern of working days or of imperative domestic arrangements can make it impossible for women to take full advantage of what seem to some to be obvious opportunities.

This brings into play a new aspect to the Univer-Cities' project: the need for players at all levels to pay more attention to being as inclusive and diverse as possible. Solutions to problems, particularly the most acute touching on inequalities, are rarely imposed successfully from above: they need input from society as research, learning and development move along, and they need voluntary and positive welcome as policy initiatives move towards application. Improving the quality of life, making use of the planet's resources sustainable, sharing them equitably, involve a sense of shared responsibility and of common involvement. None of this is easy to recognise, let alone achieve. As Professor Borysiewicz said in the Opening Address to the fourth Univer-Cities conference:

"The [previous] meetings have been extraordinarily interesting and stimulating, not least because of the broad view they have taken of the relationship between universities and the cities, regions, nations, and international communities they serve. And the comparative material has been of particular value — based mainly on what has been happening in Cambridge, Singapore, and California, but with significant insights from Australia, Hong Kong, Malaysia and Zurich. The next step is to set up a small number of focussed research projects to tackle particularly aspects of these matters."

About the Author

Gordon Johnson was formerly Deputy Vice Chancellor of the University of Cambridge, President of Wolfson College, and Chair of the Governing Body of Cambridge University Press.

CHAPTER FIVE

BERKELEY AS A CATALYST FOR A REVIVED PUBLIC REALM

RICHARD BENDER, EMILY B. MARTHINSEN AND JOHN J. PARMAN

"Since 2008, state legislatures have cut approximately $14 billion in funding from public universities, or approximately 20 percent. In 2008, President Obama asked Congress for $12 billion to revitalize the nation's community-college system. He didn't get it. But between 2013 and 2018, a lone American university — already the richest in the world — raised $9.6 billion in a single fund-raising campaign."

Tara Westover, New York Times, 29 September 2019

California's mid-20th century was a heady moment when International Style modernism, brought here by Europeans like Rudolf Schindler and Richard Neutra, mixed with the home-grown regionalism of the West Coast. It ushered in California's boom decades, through the 1960s, that saw new University of California (U.C.) Campuses built and the Bay Region's BART transit system put in. There is still a fascination with mid-century modernism in the U.S., but the Bay Region has other traditions to draw on — and a reputation for iconoclasm. Wherever it goes next, we can depend on this being a contentious, drawn-out, and imaginative process.

As we write this, a new mid-century is just a bit more than a generation away. Inequality is now a defining, across-the-board issue for the Bay Region, a problem of scarcity amid abundance, exacerbated by a tiered economy whose disparities in wealth, so visible on our urban streets, are fuelling a movement to rein in its excesses and address shortages and inequities. As in most democracies, this is a messy, politicised process.

Tackling the structural problems exemplified by the region's lack of fiscal autonomy and its unequal tax regime requires political will. But it also requires a widely shared vision of its public realm as a viable and thriving framework.

Horst Rittel, a U.C. Berkeley Professor and polymath, noted how the issues that dog the public realm are interconnected, each manifestation a symptom of a larger failing. Thus, homelessness is tied to decades of chronically low housing production, but also to the way mental illness lost its public funding and treatment facilities, the privatisation of public space, the fraying of the public safety net, and the steady loss of housing options at the margins. Homelessness is now a category, the subject of programmes that soak up considerable public and philanthropic monies. It has spawned businesses, some of which resemble or even overlap private prison providers. In a similar way, education has a grey zone of for-profit operators, organised around lacunae in the way public and private education work. Every inconsistency is an opportunity to fill the gap, but gap-filling is often an expensive and unsatisfactory workaround: not always, but too often.

"Start where you are," the Buddhists say. Berkeley as campus and community are the seeds of an ecosystem that proliferates across the Bay Region to form the public realm as a framework and rethink how it provides the goods, services, and settings that are basic to liveability. It isn't our responsibility to solve the region's problems, but to show how such problems could be solved by approaching them holistically, not challenging the multiplicity of current and future institutions, enterprises, groups, and individuals involved, but linking them as an ecosystem. This would then be a network that becomes accustomed to tackling its problems cooperatively, looking past existing boundaries to ask if there's a larger problem that needs tackling, and combining political will with enough shared vision of the outcomes to preserve liveability and urbanity — the qualities that make the Bay Region uniquely what it is — and bring them forward as defining features.

Introduction

This is our third essay for the Univer-Cities Conference series. In 2013, we considered U.C. Berkeley's past, present, and future as a leading public university in a community, Berkeley, that was founded not long before its establishment. In 2016, we looked at the roles played by U.C. Berkeley, U.C. San Francisco, and Stanford in making the Bay Region a global centre for research and innovation in science and technology. Arguing for closer collaboration among them, we noted how the lack of investment in infrastructure has hindered the growth of new centres and made intercity movement slow and cumbersome. Unless addressed, we wrote, these deficits will make the region less and less attractive — and competitive — as a global R&D centre.

Our previous essays took note of U.C. Berkeley's origins as a Land Grant College, an 1862 Act of Congress aimed at extending public higher education across the country and applying scientific and technological research to the pillars of its economy — agriculture, manufacturing, and mining. The ideal of the public university, rooted in the Land Grant College Act, has had remarkable and surprising staying power at U.C. Berkeley, despite a steady decline in state funding. This "origin story" is pertinent to the issues of inequality raised by the 2019 Univer-Cities Conference.

U.C. Berkeley is guided by a mission that was set at its founding. Along with institutional goals, this self-defining exercise took in the community around it, acknowledging and privileging their interconnectedness. One of its founding assumptions was that it would play an outsized role in creating and influencing the public realm. U.C. Berkeley has always been more than just a physical campus set within a community. From the start, it was intended to shape the cultural, economic, political, and social landscape of the state and region. Exempted from local control by this broader mandate, U.C. Berkeley has grown to its current size and stature. This has made for an unequal and often uneasy marriage with the city around it. At a time of rising inequality, however, their ability to act in tandem is an advantage. As we argue, it may make them a potential model for other universities and colleges as they tackle inequality.

The public realm is a *spatially-defined framework* of publicly accessible goods and services. It typically includes education, healthcare, housing, and transit — their availability and affordability are two measures of societal equity. In the U.S., this framework is delivered by a patchwork of organisations, public and private, funded and administered in multiple ways. In the Bay Region, only transit answers to a nascent public authority. Within this schema, higher education is part of a larger category that also takes in childcare; primary and secondary education; job-and-career-related education and training; and adult education and lifelong learning.

The Bay Region's universities and colleges — public and private alike — emphasise the value of their immediate and larger settings. The idea of a campus as a real place persists as a focal point of plans for consolidation, redevelopment, and expansion. Campuses impact the public realm, positively and negatively, and vice versa. U.C. Berkeley, with a daytime population of 50,000 people, tries to be a good neighbour to the city around it, but the shortcomings of the Bay Region's public realm make this harder — a situation shared by other institutions as they consider their longer-term prospects, and also of course by their host cities.

Higher Education as a Public Good

Higher education provided opportunities for individuals and, importantly, the places where they lived and worked, to grow and prosper. Higher education in the U.S. provided a path out of poverty and out of the working class for generations of immigrants, formerly enslaved people, and others. Colleges and universities varied greatly, of course, in assets and resources, but overall, a college education was a ticket to opportunity in the United States for most of the 20th century. Towns and cities, large and small, with colleges and universities benefited economically and culturally from their presence. University and college towns are well-liked; and, as recently as the 2008 financial crisis and its aftermath, they have weathered economic ups and downs successfully.

But inequality is now part of higher education's narrative. Student homelessness and crushing debt grab the headlines, but at an average cost of $50,000 or more per year, it is a challenging expense for middle-class families that are ineligible for financial aid. A college education is also increasingly viewed as a private good — an opportunity for individual growth, decoupled from positive community impact. Despite the long-term career benefit of higher education, a growing portion of the American public no longer sees it as a surefire route to social mobility. To address these issues and return higher education to its broader societal mandate, it is timely to reconsider it as an ecosystem.

To do so, we have to look beyond the conventional focus on individual institutions and their campuses. Because U.C. Berkeley is part of a 10-campus system, our 2013 essay nodded to this statewide network. Its importance to the Bay Region as a global research centre led us, in 2016, to ask how greater cooperation with Stanford and U.C. San Francisco could support that claim.

In our view, higher education is a key component of the framework that constitutes the public realm of every metropolis. We should therefore think of it as an *ecosystem* that includes universities, colleges, academies, centres, and schools that award post-secondary certificates and degrees. Large and small, public and private, distinguished and ordinary, they form the "universe" that employs faculty and attracts students to the region, as well as contributing to its economy. We tend to think of universities in terms of the top-tier institutions, but they are typically a fraction of what this and other metropolitan regions offer. An ecosystem including all of them as an interconnected regional network raises their collective value as a public good.

That higher education is an ecosystem was anticipated by a 1956 compact that organised public higher education in California into three tiers: the U.C. System; the California State University (C.S.U.) System; and the California Community College System. The private side includes large institutions like the California Institute of Technology, the University of Southern California, and Stanford, and smaller ones focused on liberal arts, art, design, and other fields. There are also sectarian and women's colleges. In the Bay Region alone, there are four public universities, numerous public community colleges, and a wide range of private universities, colleges, academies, conservatories, and schools — a diverse network that shares the challenge of excelling as a public good in a climate of rising costs and growing inequality.

Blurring the Distinctions

In the U.S., we often begin discussing higher education by distinguishing between public and private universities. Yet the bright line that separated the two is becoming less distinct. Public and private now best describes their historic foundations and, up to a point, their governance. Changes, notably in how both types of institutions are funded, suggest more similarities than differences. Conversations at public universities throughout the U.S. echo those at U.C. Berkeley: the amount of funding from the state has so diminished that, per a previous Chancellor, it may no longer be accurate to call U.C. Berkeley "public" in any meaningful way.

Funding for U.C. Berkeley comes from five sources: state allocations; funded research (mainly federal); tuition and fees; philanthropy; and income from endowments and patents. A private research university like Stanford has the same funding sources but in different proportions. Even the origin stories of the two universities speak to the largesse of the Hearst and Stanford families, part of California's Gold Rush aristocracy. U.C. Berkeley is a bargain for undergraduates, but elite private universities in the U.S. like Stanford use their huge endowments to ensure some diversity in their student bodies. While different, the two institutions are much less different than they seem. And they are growing more alike.

They also share a sense of themselves as part of the region's public realm. They were founded to educate its best and brightest, and help generate innovation and create the wealth that would keep graduates from leaving and attract many others to join them. If U.C. Berkeley claimed to be "the Athens of the West", it was a claim in which Leland Stanford had an equal stake.

The Valley and the Green New Deal

Stanford University is closely associated with Silicon Valley, the cradle of the contemporary tech sector. U.C. Berkeley and U.C. San Francisco are metropolitan universities. U.C. Berkeley both educates the region's highly educated workforce and carries out the "pure" research that fuels innovation in sectors beyond tech alone. U.C. San Francisco combines a teaching medical centre with specialised medical research, and operates a network of clinics, as does Stanford. If there is any distinction between private Stanford and the public U.C. Campuses, it may be that the ethos of the Valley, on the one hand, and Berkeley and San Francisco, on the other, still differ.

In broad brush, the former is libertarian, influenced by Ayn Rand's brand of it from the 1960s and 1970s. Rooted in "Tech", an evolving category with global ambitions, it operates from an unwavering self-belief that is hostile and disruptive to the public realm. In particular, Silicon Valley has sought to limit taxes. Even as its founders and the companies themselves have expanded their philanthropy, its share of the tax burden of maintaining and investing in public goods and services is not equal to its impacts on them. It takes much more than it gives.

Berkeley and San Francisco, in contrast, range from liberal to socialist. They believe in the public realm, but their ability to invest in it is stymied by structural problems including a tax regime that is overdependent on real property and consumption, and gets much less funding from the Federal Government for entitlement programmes and infrastructure projects.

The Green New Deal, a policy proposal put forward by democratic socialists in the Democratic Party, speaks to the metropolitan Bay Region's Progressive ethos, which sees a strong government role — federal to local — in planning, administering, and funding the public realm as a framework of publicly accessible, affordable goods and services. To work, the Green New Deal would have to address the structural problems of California's existing tax regime, which largely exempts corporate profits and, concurrently, sees net outflows in federal taxes to other states.

These two different value systems, also reflected at the national level, are part of the context in which the higher education ecosystem in the Bay Region operates. They help explain why an economy the size of the Netherlands can neither provide nor invest in public goods and services at the same level. Singapore could be a model, but the region lacks Singapore's political autonomy and will. Even compared to Los Angeles, whose city-county government maps its metropolitan area closely, the Bay Region lacks a political centre. While there are efforts to form one by combining the transit authority with a new entity focused on housing, the closest thing to a regional political power is a working coalition of Bay Area state legislators. They are pushing legislation to override local controls on housing production and impose limits on rents. While aimed at a headline manifestation of inequality in the region and the lack of affordable housing, these measures target perceived roadblocks rather than increasing public investment and subsidies.

Higher education is affected by these shortcomings. As an ecosystem, potentially with pre-school, primary, and secondary education in its purview, it has opportunities to address them. By acting in concert to find collective solutions, it could show cities and counties in the region how to cooperate for the same purpose. As stewards of the region's future, it could exercise moral suasion, mediating between advocates for the two ethos who are often at loggerheads.

Evolving Berkeley's Own Ecosystem

Before they can generate a wider ecosystem, U.C. Berkeley and the City of Berkeley both need to take concrete steps to firm up their own. They won't be starting from scratch. Despite the friction inherent in any long relationship, their ties and interdependence continue. We foresee four steps that would build on them and turn a nascent ecosystem into a real one.

Step One: Campus–Community Cooperation: Our 2013 essay looked at Berkeley as an archetypal university city. The two grew up together. In the spirit of *modus vivendi*, the university has steadily expanded its cooperation with the city in recent years, doing more institutionally to address its impacts, especially on the west and south sides of campus.

The jointly developed Downtown Area Plan (DAP) makes Center Street the pedestrian entry to the campus from the west, connecting to the city's main transit station. U.C. Berkeley and the city both contributed to BART's recent renovation of the station plaza. More important, DAP raised the overall density and broadened the mix of uses downtown, positioning the university as a major partner in its redevelopment. The decision to move the University Art Museum and Pacific Film Archive to Center Street, across from campus and a block from transit, underlined the area's importance as a cultural and tourist destination, accessible from across the region.

New university buildings clustered north of University Avenue and east of Shattuck Avenue are expanding downtown Berkeley as a mixed, walkable, urban-scale academic, commercial, cultural, and residential district. The newest academic building houses classrooms, offices, and research facilities for Education, Psychology, and Public Health. All three have community-focused programmes that benefit from the building's close proximity to transit. Ground-floor retail serves the academic community and nearby residents, filling in a gap in the gourmet corridor along Shattuck Avenue to the north, anchored by Alice Water's Chez Panisse. The building has leasable Class A office space — in short supply in Berkeley — to fill out its academic programme. The decision to build the additional space honours DAP's commitment to higher density. It contrasts with a nearby "surge" building that, at three storeys, only met the university's immediate need.

The south entrance to campus, Sproul Plaza, has been redeveloped to support a student body that lives and works in new ways. Moffitt Library, the main undergraduate library, which terminates the campus' south entry sequence, has been similarly transformed to support new ways of learning. The library is as much about meeting and conferring with peers as it is about supporting individual study. Research librarians are there to help students navigate a world of online, digitised resources or request books and journals from offsite storage. Amazon has an outlet in Sproul Plaza that provides safe delivery of goods, separate from students' housing.

Between the campus edge and Dwight Way, five blocks south, the university has added housing on its own and with partners. Following a fire that destroyed an older apartment building on the Telegraph Avenue corridor, the university took a master lease in the redeveloped property to help its private owner secure financing. Fifty years after the turmoil that led to People's Park, the university and the city will replace it with student and homeless housing, a move strongly supported by the surrounding district and its Council representative, although not without controversy among "old lefties" in the community. The university owns the land and is legally free to develop it as it chooses, but it chose to work cooperatively for resolution. And vice versa, of course — trust has been steadily built by mutual planning and follow-through.

For its part, the community has passed bond measures to invest in affordable housing. How the money is spent is decided by citizen commissions that include former campus planning staff, familiar to the Mayor and Council as co-authors of the joint plans now being implemented.

The current faculty is engaged as advisers — the Terner Center, for example, weighs in on housing. These relationships are longstanding but informal, reflecting the porosity of town and gown.

Step 2: The Community-Serving Campus: Higher education across the Bay Region has a range of "campus" models. Stanford, like Berkeley, grew around a historic core of older buildings and formal open spaces. U.C. San Francisco added a separate research campus to augment its original Parnassus Heights home. California College of the Arts (CCA) is shifting from its small, venerable campus off College Avenue in Oakland, south of U.C. Berkeley to an urban campus in a former industrial area in San Francisco below Potrero Hill and west of Mission Bay. Academy of Art University is even more dispersed across the city, while the San Francisco Art Institute has opened a second facility at Fort Mason, a new arts-and-culture anchor in the Marina District.

The sheer variety of types weighs against the idea of a campus as a "world apart". The range of students served and the forms their access takes are blurring the boundaries still further. U.C. Berkeley's 178-acre campus reflects the tiered, real-and-virtual nature of the boundary. You need a card or an email address for entry to parts of it, but a growing cohort of others is accommodated, for a fee or as a public good. Despite decades of active, changing use, the campus still reads as a park. This reflects the deft hands of its early planners and its founding campus architect. With its west entry a short walk from regional transit, this is a place people visit, whether or not they have formal ties to the university. Even as it blends into the districts that adjoin it, the campus setting, with its Beaux Arts monuments, defines the community.

Following the recommendations of the Campus Planning Study Group, set down in the early 1980s, U.C. Berkeley began to develop the central campus at a generally higher density and, when possible, make more intensive use of existing buildings through redevelopment and a variety of revenue-generating activities beyond the daytime, full-time academic programme.

The Berkeley campus has long been an important regional destination for performing arts and intercollegiate athletic competitions. Zellerbach Hall, its main concert hall and playhouse, opened in 1968. It brings world-known artists and their audiences to the Berkeley campus. Hertz Hall and the Berkeley Art Museum and Pacific Film Archive are also popular cultural destinations, augmented by year-round art-and-culture workshops and summer camps. Cal's football stadium and basketball arena draw thousands of alumni and fans. Its aquatic centre and track stadium host high-school and well as university events.

On the academic side, long-time professional and continuing education programmes like those of the Haas School of Business and U.C. Berkeley Extension are now accompanied by career development, degree, and certificate programmes that connect U.C. Berkeley to a wider network of higher education in the region. Campus/community interaction has grown in importance. U.C. Berkeley's Osher Lifelong Learning Institute (OLLI) runs a four-quarter programme of short courses for "inquiring adults", most in settings beyond the campus. BAMPFA, the university's art museum, hosts academic courses with weekly public lectures. The nearby Magnes Museum, newly acquired by the University, also hosts joint events related to its collection and mission.

Some U.C. Berkeley activities make use of facilities at other campuses, beginning to create a kind of physical network for the higher education ecosystem that we describe. Shared facilities like the Stanford Linear Accelerator are well-known, but Cal's hockey team has used Stanford's fields to practise and play, while some Cal students are housed in Holy Names University dorms in Oakland. This pattern of shared use is likely to grow as the higher education ecosystem looks to its members and beyond them to find housing, theatre venues, clinical and research space, and other facilities that serve their own needs and those of the wider community.

Step Three: Public Education as a Network: U.C. and C.S.U. shape the academic side of the California Community College System by setting the requirements and standards for transfer and advancement to upper division status. The U.C. System has made a point of fostering this relationship to further its goals for student diversity and equality of access. If there is an argument for expanding California's education ecosystem to address its quality fully and consciously from pre-school on up, these two goals are at the heart of it. Below the university level, the public institutions involved are tied to their communities, with wide variation in their resources and quality of outcomes; private schools are tied to their sponsors. To recast them as an eco-system would leave much to the traditions and prerogatives of its member institutions, but deal systemically with their limiting factors.

Of these factors, inequality of access to resources across public K–12 education stands out. For most families the tradeoffs are between housing costs and school quality. Affluent suburbs have strong, well-funded public schools. Many urban communities have a mix of good public schools and bad, while some have no good public schools at all. To the extent that parents face shortages or an outright lack of good public schools, their children's futures are endangered. This has a cascading impact on the regional economy, crimping the social mobility that higher education makes possible by shutting whole cohorts of young people from its potential ranks.

An interesting example for higher education's involvement in public K–12 education is Ball State University's partnership with the Muncie, Indiana, Community Schools. Ball State University is a state university, founded in Muncie in 1918, with 22,500 students. Muncie, a post-industrial city of 70,000 people, is a regional healthcare centre for east central Indiana. Its public schools were in sufficient crisis that the State of Indiana took control of them in 2018. By mutual agreement, the university formed a partnership with the city's schools, appointing a new board, embarking on an academic innovation plan for the K–12 programme, developed jointly with schools, to be completed in 2020. With public and foundation funding, the programme is envisioned as a testbed for new ideas and initiatives in K–12 education. The private University of Chicago's Laboratory Schools, founded in 1896 by the educator-philosopher John Dewey, is an earlier precedent.

Currently, students in their last two years at Berkeley High School can take courses at the university if their academic programmes warrant it. The one lab-type activity U.C. Berkeley maintains is the Harold E. Jones Child Study Center, founded in 1927. One of the oldest such centres in the U.S., its childcare programme, in a facility designed by the AIA Gold Medalist Joseph Esherick, gives priority to the university community, but also serves community residents.

A clear opportunity for Berkeley, campus and community, is to expand these relationships. U.C. Berkeley is heavily involved in Berkeley's Vision 2020 Initiative, which addresses public schools. Since 2005, its School of Education has partnered with Aspire Public Schools, a non-profit charter management organisation, to run Richmond Aspire California College Preparatory Academy in nearby Richmond, California. Aspire operates 40 public charter schools in California and Tennessee. Berkeley Unified School District's autonomy from the City of Berkeley means that any new initiatives involving the city's public schools would need its participation. Vision 2020 suggests that the Berkeley community would welcome their expansion.

Inequality as a Societal Leitmotif

Inequality is part of higher education's narrative. In her 29 September 2019 *New York Times* review of *The Years that Matter Most* by Paul Tough, Tara Westover writes,

> We are divided economically and politically, and education sits conspicuously at the center of both divides. Whether you have a college degree turns out to be one of the strongest predictors of your political preferences and your income. Reading Tough's book, you cannot fail to notice that we have allowed the inequities of our economic system to be reproduced in our education system. We then ask ourselves why so many Americans no longer believe in college or degrees, why they perceive education as not for them but rather as a good distributed by the elites to elites. **The answer is straightforward: If we want others to believe in public education, we first have to believe in it ourselves.**

Higher education's issues of inequality reflect larger ones in the U.S. symptomatic of the disparities created by the unequal distribution of wealth and of access to basic goods, services, and settings. A narrative of inequality across society has become a leitmotif that seems to defy resolution. If established politicians here are in trouble, it is in large part because their standard solutions only address parts of the problem while leaving the rest untouched or worse.

In her 1998 essay, "Community Property", U.C. Los Angeles Professor Dana Cuff made the point that the redevelopment of post-industrial sites, tapping public funds and subsidies, is a flawed model. Such projects — Manhattan's Hudson Yards is the latest U.S. example — are still held out as a valid way for metropolitan regions to revive the public realm. In a 1970 interview, George Candilis, the late planner of the Mirail redevelopment project in Toulouse, argued that 20 years is too short to transform the urban fabric in the way such projects propose to do. Whatever is built so quickly risks becoming prematurely obsolete — a phenomenon already visible in China. More important, these projects invest public money in essentially private goods. The model is tipped towards corporate and individual beneficiaries, another instance of elites serving elites.

To support the public realm as a broadly accessible framework, it has to be insulated from the distorting effects of private capital seeking immediate returns and targeting the wealthy. Candilis was right: 20 years is nothing in the evolution of a city — too brief to subject private and public interests to longer-term measures of value. Success for developers is mainly financial, with affordability and public access kept to the mini-mum needed to obtain planning approvals.

The bankruptcy of the model in larger terms reflects a public interest that has consistently been too narrowly served. The appearance of such "externalities" as inequality and environmental degradation is a warning signal that is currently flashing brightly. And yet redevelopment is still held out as a valid model for improving the public realm: "progress" given speculative form and sold on that basis, now with state laws to force its approval at the community level — laws enacted in the name of afford-ability, by legislators who believe the public realm will benefit.

The Univer-City as an Alternate Model

Part of the power of the U.C. Berkeley Campus is its ability to inspire people. The vast majority of it is publicly accessible, part of the public realm in a broad rather than a narrow sense. From the outset, it was intended as a long-lived, open-ended framework. Its most important feature is that it can evolve, reflecting time and experience, even as it adheres to foundational values.

In light of this, Daniel Burnham's famous maxim should be, "Make no *narrow* plans".

The campus and community fit and work together synergistically, but they also form a larger whole that is "alive" and responsive to change. This may still be more their potential than their reality, but they are nonetheless a good place to try things out — a seedbed and a laboratory. This is recognisably an extension of its founding purpose — the same idea that, on the private side, led to Leland Stanford's public-spirited gift of his namesake university in honour of his son. It reconnects higher education in the Bay Region to the public realm in a new way, making use of its unique position as a unifier of such opposites as public and private or research and career.

The U.C. Berkeley Campus has banners that ask, "Remember when no one lived to be 120?" Seeing a different future is why you want higher education in your midst — to spark the public imagination to anticipate positive change and support its realisation. Awareness of how the interconnectedness of the public realm makes it stronger is the other reason. Walter Hood, a Professor of Landscape Architecture at U.C. Berkeley, just won a MacArthur Grant for a career devoted to showing how place and community transform each other, empowered by a mutual understanding that builds trust and makes collective, long-term action possible.

A univer-city like Berkeley is a catalyst for transformation, as Hood grasped early on. His grant is for genius, and the Spirit of the Place is also honoured. Inequality is felt most acutely as a lack of access to vitally needed public goods and as a future constricted by too narrow a view. At a time when the young take the old to task for failing them, rebalancing the public realm through education and example is the heart of the matter. **It's called "higher education" for a reason.**

About the Authors

Richard Bender is Former Professor of Architecture and Dean Emeritus, College of Environmental Design, University of California, Berkeley.

Emily B. Marthinsen, FAIA is Campus Architect and Assistant Vice-Chancellor for Physical and Environment Planning emerita, University of California, Berkeley.

John J. Parman is a Visiting Scholar in Architecture at the University of California, Berkeley.

CHAPTER SIX

MEETING SOCIETAL CHALLENGES THROUGH MEDICAL EDUCATION AND RESEARCH: LKCMEDICINE, NTU-ICL SINGAPORE

JAMES BEST

Introduction

Medical Schools are complex entities and incorporating a new medical school into a relatively new and high performing university is a daunting task. In 2001, when Nanyang Technological University (NTU) was only ten years old, it was not considered ready to embark on this venture, particularly as it had not established a firm base in the biological sciences. By 2010, the landscape had changed and the Singapore Prime Minister announced the establishment of a new Medical School to be located within NTU, in partnership with Imperial College London (ICL).

This change of heart occurred because NTU had broadened its academic base, both in the sciences and the arts, while retaining its key strength in engineering, with a strong academic emphasis also on business. At the same time, there was increasing recognition of the medical workforce needs of a rapidly ageing population in Singapore, with a low birth rate and limited immigration. There were of course two existing Medical Schools, both associated with the National University of Singapore (NUS). The Yong Loo Lin School of Medicine (NUS Medicine) was established over 100 years ago and admits around 300 students annually to a five-year MBBS programme. Formally established in 2005, the graduate entry Duke-NUS Medical School provides a four-year MD programme, modelled on the Duke University course in the US. The option was to increase the size of the existing Schools or to create a new one: the Singapore Government chose the latter option.

Another reason for establishing a third Medical School in Singapore was that, due to the limited number of medical student places locally, many Singaporean students chose to study medicine overseas. Singapore also needed to recruit doctors internationally because of the shortfall in meeting its needs from local graduates. The goals were to allow more Singaporean students to study medicine in Singapore and for Singapore to become self-sufficient in developing its own medical workforce. At the same time, NTU was undergoing an academic overhaul — that would lead to a spectacular rise in the international rankings — and remained keen to establish a Medical School.

Birth of a Medical School

This background is important, because it defined the rationale for the School and established the need for it to be distinctive, to have a different personality to the existing Schools. The decision for NTU to have an international partner and the choice of Imperial College London as the School's other parent were key strategies to set a high benchmark. This approach also provided a model of a university with strength in Engineering, Technology and Business, which had itself acquired a Medical School, albeit one that was well established, only in 1988. Many Singaporeans had studied at Imperial, particularly engineering, and Imperial is a highly regarded brand with a strong alumni base in Singapore.

The then Minister for Education, Dr Ng Eng Hen, is quoted as saying he wanted a Medical School with "different DNA" pointing out that DNA is derived from both parents. The School's vision of "*Redefining medicine and transforming healthcare*" sets an ambitious goal, that again asks the School to be different.

While the agreement to establish a joint Medical School was signed by the partners in 2010, the first students (54 in number) were admitted in 2013. At this time, Bertil Andersson was President of NTU and was a driving force behind the establishment of the School. Since he presented at the 2016 Univer-Cities Conference, three groups of students have graduated and are working in the Singapore healthcare system. We now admit 150 students per year.

My own journey with the Lee Kong Chian School of Medicine (LKCMedicine) started in mid-2014, in time to welcome the second cohort of students. Bertil Andersson kept a close eye on LKCMedicine until the conclusion of his term as NTU President at the end of 2017. LKCMedicine has many stakeholders including NTU and Imperial. The School is directly overseen by a Governing Board, with representation from NTU, Imperial, the Singapore Ministries of Education and Health, as well as our key clinical partner, National Healthcare Group (NHG). We are embedded in NTU, following virtually all NTU regulations and participating in all activities, while maintaining a close connection with Imperial. Our London-based parent has strong oversight of the MBBS course, with increasing partnership in research. It is a complex environment in which to operate, with a robust governance system and wide-ranging support for all our activities, that has ensured success.

Recruitment of outstanding Faculty, both locally and internationally, has been an essential element for the School's progress. Initially, senior international Faculty members, including several from Imperial, were recruited to develop the research and education programmes and to mentor early career Faculty as they were recruited over time. NTU's Nanyang Assistant Professor scheme was particularly helpful in attracting exceptional early career Faculty from around the world.

Distinctiveness in Medical Education

The primary mission of a Medical School is of course to educate future doctors and having a clear view of the kind of doctor we want to produce has formulated key aspects of our pedagogy. As our mission statement indicates, LKCMedicine wants to produce doctors "*who advance the science and practice of medicine for the good of humanity, the doctors you and I would like to have caring for us*". In meeting the needs of the society of which we are part, this goal includes: addressing the needs of an ageing population; preparing for the era of precision medicine, mega data and AI; and practising medicine with humility, integrity and compassion. These are diverse requirements and developing the knowledge, skills and attitudes of our student doctors is a demanding task. It is easy to overlook the third of these categories and leave it up to the "hidden" curriculum, so we make a particular effort to address matters of the heart as well as those of the head.

A forward-looking and distinctive curriculum was developed in a three-way partnership between an education team based at Imperial, LKCMedicine faculty and clinician-educators from NHG. There is a major component of IT-enabled team-based learning in the first two years of the curriculum and throughout the course professionalism, wellbeing, collegiality/teamwork have been emphasised. We are confident about the standards we have set, because of the partnership with Imperial and our use of external local and international examiners in all years of the course.

Our system of allocating students to one of five "houses" for the duration of their course, with house tutors able to provide individual and longitudinal attention to students, reinforces all of the qualities we want our students to display. For a new Medical School without an alumni base or illustrious history to draw upon, establishment of the ethos or culture we want for the School is also supported by an emphasis on the School's values of Humility, Integrity, Compassion, Continuous Learning and Professionalism.

While not in any way restricting the career choices open to our students after graduation, we have sought to reinforce the Ministry of Health's support for Family Medicine as a key component of the medical workforce. We have recruited a Professor of Family Medicine and Primary Care, appointed Family Doctors as Assistant Deans and made Family Medicine one of three rotations in our Student Assistantship Programme that is placed just prior to graduation.

To continue our goal of an innovative medical curriculum, while ensuring rigorous evaluation of novel methods, we have appointed a Professor of Medical Education and Research. Our interest in digital education has been extended internationally, particularly through a collaboration with the WHO, resulting in being designated as a WHO Collaborating Centre for Digital Health and Health Education in 2019. (See <http://www.lkcmedicine.ntu.edu.sg/Research/WHOCC/Pages/home.aspx>.)

Contributing to Biomedical Science, Clinical and Population Health Research

It was essential that a Medical School formed as a partnership between two research-intensive universities should have a strong emphasis on research. At the same time, Singapore already had a vibrant research environment, with the two existing Medical Schools forming Academic Medical Centres with their healthcare partners and an extensive, multi-faceted research agency A*STAR (Agency for Science, Technology and Research). While the education agenda had clear goals and timelines, the research programme was open-ended and it was up to the School to map it out.

One guiding principle for the research programme was to emphasise collaboration with our primary healthcare partner NHG and with other Schools at NTU. Our Clinical Sciences Building in central Singapore is next to the National Centre for Infectious Diseases, both part of Health City Novena, which includes NHG's flagship Tan Tock Seng Hospital and the National Skin Centre. We have worked closely with NHG to develop joint research programmes, leveraging on NHG's clinical capabilities. Based on the NTU campus in West Jurong, our Experimental Medicine Building provides the opportunity to pursue more fundamental research and to partner with other NTU Schools, initially those in the College of Engineering and College of Science.

We have also established excellent collaborations with colleagues at Imperial, with A*STAR and the other Singapore Medical Schools, as well as with other Medical Schools internationally. These partnerships take time to develop and need to be based on having something to offer the potential partner. For a university or a healthcare system that is not used to conducting research with a medical school as part of a strategic partnership, trust and respect must be earned over time.

One excellent example of a major collaborative research programme with NHG and Imperial is the population-based HELIOS (Health for Life in Singapore) study. HELIOS is a state-of-the-art prospective population-based epidemiological study. The study aims to identify the genetic and environmental factors that underpin development of obesity, diabetes, cardiovascular disease and other complex diseases in Singapore. The ultimate goal is to develop new approaches for prediction, prevention, early detection and better treatment for these chronic diseases.

Another principle for our new Medical School was to identify areas of research that were not already well covered within the existing local research ecosystem and which were of national significance. Initial recruitment of senior faculty was essential for establishing the research base, followed by a strong emphasis on recruiting early career scientists, many for their first faculty positions. While about a third of our faculty have qualified in medicine, the majority have a background in science, particularly those at early career stage.

Our strong teaching partnership with NHG to produce the next generation of clinicians is complemented by our joint efforts to develop clinician scientists. We work together as partners in the Clinician Scientist Development Committee to encourage and support early career clinicians who want to make research a significant part of their medical careers. We have made more than 10 joint appointments of clinicians who have been successful in the National Medical Research Council clinician scientist funding schemes. We have also enrolled over 20 clinicians for PhD studies. The programme has enjoyed strong support from the NHG Board and senior management.

Some areas where we have achieved successful research partnerships are in Neuroscience and Mental Health; Infectious Diseases and Respiratory Medicine; Population Health (incorporating cardiovascular disease, cancer and diabetes, as well as family medicine); Neuroscience and Mental Health; Regenerative, Restorative and Rehabilitation Medicine (incorporating wound healing aspects of dermatology and ageing). Partners include NHG entities such as the National Centre for Infectious Diseases, Institute of Mental Health, National Skin Centre and NHG Polyclinics; NTU Schools of Biological Sciences, Chemical and Biomedical Engineering, Material Science and Engineering, Computer Science and Engineering, Social Sciences; A*STAR institutes such as the Institute for Molecular and Cell Biology, Institute of Medical Biology and Genome Institute of Singapore. With Imperial we collaborate in the study of infectious diseases, neuroscience, respiratory medicine, population health, diabetes and metabolism.

Blending research and education, rather than having these two mandates as parallel streams is another ongoing task. Co-location of education and research functions in both the Clinical Sciences Building and the Experimental Medicine Building enhances the opportunity for interaction. For all our students to appreciate how new knowledge is generated we have included a full-time six-week block at the start of year 4. Titled the Scholarly Project, students choose between four areas:

Laboratory and Translational Research, Medical Education, Medical Practice, and Medicine and Society. Students report on the outcome of their projects in the format of a scientific paper and many students continue to work on projects after the full-time period, resulting in presentation at meetings and co-authorship of publications. Supervision of the project can be undertaken by LKCMedicine Faculty, NHG clinicians or NTU Faculty from other Schools, particularly in the College of Engineering. Supported by the Anthony SC Teo — Gordon Johnson Scholarship, students will be able to conduct their Scholarly Project while based at Wolfson College, Cambridge. In coming years we plan to expand the number of students who are able to travel to overseas universities for their Scholarly Project.

Further approaches to research-led education include ensuring all of our Faculty are involved in teaching for the MBBS programme. This approach also provides an opportunity for our Faculty to offer a glimpse of their research activities to our students. In the other direction, we have emphasised medical education research and are promoting links with the National Institute of Education Singapore (part of NTU), as well as other NTU entities, and with NHG, which has a Health Outcomes and Medical Education Research (HOMER) Unit.

Challenges and Opportunities

With three sets of medical graduates, there is a challenge to maintain the initial fervour and excitement that came with a new Medical School. At the same time, having proven ourselves as able to produce high quality doctors, there is an opportunity to continue to innovate and to share bi-directionally with Imperial novel approaches to medical education. There may also be an opportunity to develop some joint postgraduate courses for online or mixed methods delivery.

Medicine is a course where 60% of the curriculum is delivered in the workplace, across multiple healthcare institutions throughout Singapore by many hundreds of clinician teachers. It is an ongoing task nurturing these multiple partnerships and maintaining standards for our pedagogical model, while explaining to NTU the difference from other Schools which operate predominantly from the one campus with full-time faculty.

In research, one of the challenges is to focus and build on existing strengths, while looking for new opportunities. We have made a good start, but have a long way to go in developing strategic collaborations, particularly with other Medical Schools internationally. We have some excellent interactions based on the efforts of individual faculty, but apart from Imperial, we do not have any systematic, co-ordinated, multi-stranded partnerships. Again, we must be careful to focus on a few quality relationships.

Ten years from signing an agreement is not long to establish a joint Medical School, given the complexities of an international partnership, which is an unusual arrangement, compared with the more usual offshore Medical School model. If we use the analogy of a sigmoid curve to display the stage of development, I believe LKCMedicine is on the straight line upward trajectory, with great potential to move onwards and upwards in the coming years.

About the Author

James Best is NTU President's Chair in Medicine, Professor and Dean of the Lee Kong Chian School of Medicine, a Joint Medical School of the Nanyang Technological University, Singapore and Imperial College London.

Fig. 6.1. The graduation of LKCMedicine's first student cohort in 2018 was a major milestone for the School.

Fig. 6.2. The White Coat Ceremony forms an important part of LKCMedicine's focus on the development of a professional identity. In 2019, the School admitted 150 students.

Fig. 6.3. Outstanding early career Faculty have been recruited locally and internationally, with significant support from the Nanyang Assistant Professor (NAP) scheme.

Fig. 6.4. IT-enabled team-based learning (TBL) is the cornerstone for delivery of the integrated curriculum in the first two years of the MBBS course.

LKCMedicine House System

LKCMedicine's comprehensive House System allocates personal House Tutors to individual students for guidance and mentorship. Students are assigned to one of five Houses at the start of their studies and remain in the same House throughout their time at LKCMedicine. Students and their House Tutors meet regularly as a group and also in one-to-one meetings.

The House Tutors guide students to develop their understanding of higher education, the curriculum, the demands of the medical profession and the satisfaction of achieving their academic, personal and professional goals.

To inspire the medical students, the five LKCMedicine Houses are named after historical figures who have had an impact on the history and profession of Medicine.

Fig. 6.5. The LKCMedicine House System plays an important role in pastoral care and professional development for medical students.

Fig. 6.6. Official designation of LKCMedicine/NTU as host of the WHO Collaborating Centre for Digital Health and Health Education during the visit to Singapore of WHO Director-General, Dr Tedros Adhanom Ghebreyesus.

Fig. 6.7. The National Centre for Infectious Diseases (NCID) is located next to LKCMedicine's Clinical Sciences Building on the Novena Campus.

Fig. 6.8. Opening of LKCMedicine Population and Community Health Laboratories by Senior Minister of State, Department of Health, Dr Amy Khor. The HELIOS study is a key component of these laboratories, as is the Family Medicine and Primary Care team.

Fig. 6.9. Entry to the Clinical Sciences Building on the Novena Campus in 2017, completing the outstanding facilities for education and research for the new Medical School.

Fig. 6.10. The Scholarly Project at the start of the 4th year of the MBBS course provides students with a research experience, part of LKCMedicine's efforts to integrate its education and research missions.

CHAPTER SEVEN

UNIVER-CITY OF ZURICH: AN EVOLVED EVOLUTIONARY MEDICINE PERSPECTIVE*

FRANK RÜHLI AND MACIEJ HENNEBERG

Introduction

Present-day practice of anything from urban planning to treatment of a sick person often relies on platonic idealism and is focused on an individual, usually a reductionistic approach to specific phenomena. However, nature and human societies are complex and dynamic. To progress, it is crucial to have an interdisciplinary approach finding common ground of different activities by studying fundamental patterns of natural systems (humans, society, environment). In a system, any change of one of its elements influences all other elements. Dynamic systems are therefore undergoing continuous evolutionary changes. Understanding those changes, and the principles that rule them, is imperative. Here we will describe how the emergence of a small new academic discipline influences the entire system, and is influenced by it.

Academic institutions such as universities as well as human settlements as in the prototype of modern cities are both systems which are unique yet interconnected. To understand their foundation and their fundamental dynamism, an evolutionary perspective is crucial. Therefore, we approach the topic of the relationship between universities and cities from the point of view of the emerging health sciences discipline — Evolutionary Medicine. We examine both the broad theoretical level and the level of concrete examples of recent practice at two universities located at two different hemispheres.

A university is a unique organisation that cannot be likened to any commercial company, church, theatre, orchestra, hospital, nor a military regiment.

---

*This chapter represents the authors' personal view only and is not the official position of the University of Zurich or the University of Adelaide.

Academic institutions are places where interaction of human minds occurs. They work best when such interaction and development of individual intellects is cherished and supported. Since universities are located in cities, the atmosphere of a city that impacts lives of academics and students plays a role in the performance of a university, while this performance informs the life of the city. The closer this relationship, the better.

The univer-city of Zurich is thus a good model for many aspects of academia and city life. Following on from our earlier paper that appeared in Vol III of the Univer-Cities book series,[1] this chapter highlights some developments that have taken place in recent years. We also address the organisation and evaluation of academic performance and expectations.

The impact of Evolutionary Medicine and thinking related to it can be seen on all three levels: the institute, the university and the city level. New disciplines and areas of science/research arise in academia, especially where institutional structures are flexible, encourage collaborations and innovation. Universities that can "capture" new disciplines and establish their centres within institutional structures quickly, benefit themselves, the society and the city in a number of ways. The foundation of the academic field of Evolutionary Medicine and in particular its "physical" construct of the Institute at the Medical Faculty of Zurich are such an example.

Evolutionary Medicine is a rather novel field to understand the *why* and not only *how* a health problem occurs. Historically, medicine started as a practical activity to make the life of people more comfortable. This, of course included "saving lives" and repairing traumatic injuries. Medical treatment always starts from a diagnosis. This, in the past, was usually symptomatic, but has evolved to focus on the cause of the ailment. Treatment is deduced from the diagnosis: if the diagnosis is symptomatic, e.g., a headache, then the treatment is also symptomatic, viz., a pain killer. When the diagnosis discovers a cause, the treatment is aimed at removing the cause: it may be killing a pathogen causing the disease; it may be, in public health, introducing a barrier between a pathogen and patients; or advising patients to stop exposing themselves to a cause. However, with the advance of modern research one realises that human health and its disruption areoften not monocausal, not proximal and not static. All this calls for the novel field of Evolutionary Medicine. This is a more holistic, ultimate and dynamic approach. It is based on established core principles of evolutionary biology and modern clinical medicine. Evolutionary perspectives are therefore inevitably pertinent on all three levels discussed in this chapter: the institute, the university and the city.

Evolutionary Medicine Perspectives at the Institute Level

In the University of Zurich an "Institute" is an organisational unit corresponding to what may be called a department or a school at many other universities. It is a unit immediately below the Faculty, or a College. These are basic divisions of a university: university — faculty — institute. Hence a university is divided into faculties, faculties into institutes. An institute has several academics at the professorial level and is usually divided into working groups or labs lead by professors and consisting of several junior academics and a number of postgraduate students each. At Zurich's Institute of Evolutionary Medicine, the innovative character of evolutionary thinking is incorporated into all work, primarily research and teaching.

In 2010 — thanks to a successful large private funding application — it was possible to found the initial "Centre for Evolutionary Medicine" at the University of Zurich. After several years of constant growth, it eventually became the current large independent academic unit — "Institute of Evolutionary Medicine" as a part of the Medical Faculty, a worldwide "primeur", a first of its kind. Establishment of this new institute was disruptive to the traditional structure of the Faculty of Medicine for two reasons: 1. Academic staff members (and their allocated rooms) who established the Institute were formerly members of another unit. 2. The new institute had not been aligned with any traditionally recognised medical science or medical specialisation. Also, there were no real additional budgets within the faculty for the establishment of new professorships or the Institute. However, in the last few years the newly established Institute and the successful appointment of two assistant professorships in two core fields (paleogenetics and human ecology) significantly helped to broaden the disciplinary content of the Institute and its outreach. Also, the first ever Chair in Evolutionary Medicine (full professorship) in any medical faculty was established. In recent years, the Institute has had a particular outreach and impact within the local Medical Faculty.

Faculty members, especially junior scientists, are more aware of the fact that an evolutionary perspective in medicine is not only nice to have but actually it is crucial to solve clinical and scientific problems. The number of students who want to pursue postgraduate work (masters or doctorate levels) is increasing too. Finally, one sees more and more senior academics who want to be affiliated with the Institute, at least partially due to its standing as an innovative research institution. The set-up and organisation of this new Institute shows how disruption of a traditional structure of a faculty per se does not produce a negative impact. The Institute has, since its founding six years ago in 2014, shown the benefit of attracting people from around the world for collaborations and for large conferences that also have a positive impact for the economy of the city.

Evolutionary Medicine Perspectives at the University Level

There are several essential factors for the success of new institutes. These include organisation of the university as an institution, its governance processes and the academic culture it inherited and is cultivating. If we compare the two universities — University of Zurich and University of Adelaide — to which both of us as authors are affiliated, one can clearly see a different evolution of disciplinary innovation in the last decade. The University of Zurich is still — more the University of Adelaide seems to be — pursuing, though perhaps not perfectly, the idea of the university as a collegial institution run by academics, open to discussions and changes resulting from initiatives of individual academics or small groups of them. The formation of the Institute at the University of Zurich was mostly a bottom-up initiative. However, support from the faculty board as well as from the University board was obtained and the practical implementation took place at the collegial faculty level.

In comparison, at the University of Adelaide, the Wood Jones Chair of Anthropological and Comparative Anatomy endowed by an individual alumnus of this university in the 1990s, had the stated aim to follow novel lines of research in biological anthropology, especially the idea of studying ongoing human evolution. After the appointment of the founding professor to this chair, initially it worked well. However, in the last few years a more managerial university leadership took over the control of the agenda of the Academic Board, removing vestiges of academic democracy and introducing "line management". It became more difficult to grow new areas of study mostly because of micromanagement of budgets. As a result, the institution deteriorated to the status of a "provider of education" and production line of narrowly defined research projects.

To our understanding the main aim of universities is to educate future generations of bright people who can think critically and enrich human knowledge and professional practice. Therefore, the quality of universities is of utmost interest to both the public and the scholarly community. There are many attempts at evaluation of universities' "output" using methods that evaluate commercial enterprises. These, however, cannot inform us whether universities are fulfilling their core responsibilities. The work of universities is extremely diversified due to the numerous varied disciplines of knowledge their members pursue, as well as to great differences among skills required to teach the practice of various professions — compare education of musicians and veterinarians. It is extremely difficult therefore to develop objective quantitative measures of a university's performance that are uniformly comparable in enhancing improvement of tertiary education.

Based on our own unpublished results, rankings of the "top 100" universities globally are based on their reputation as gathered by public surveys. The reputation is mostly based on subjective opinions of academics, students and the public. Student full-time-equivalent numbers, staff numbers, student/staff ratios, staff numbers, female/male student ratios, percentage of international students, percentage of income from the industry, total budgets and budgets per staff member are all factors explaining only minor parts of a university's reputation. It follows that strategic decisions regarding work of universities (e.g., research, student and staff numbers) should be internally based on the broad input of academics and students (variously called Academic Boards, Senates, Regent House). Only collegial academic governance based on broad internal democracy can ensure that an institution is run well and will flourish. This self-evident principle clashes with the ideology of managerial rationalism which dictates that the university manager should make decisions based on economic calculations and simply "buy" academics with the best metric indicators of their productivity. Fostering innovative intellectual work in a university rather than micromanagement based on formal quantitative indices can improve its worldwide rankings faster than large investments into complex administrative structures and new buildings. The best intellectual work takes place in an atmosphere of academic freedom from top-down management and collegiality of relations among staff and students.

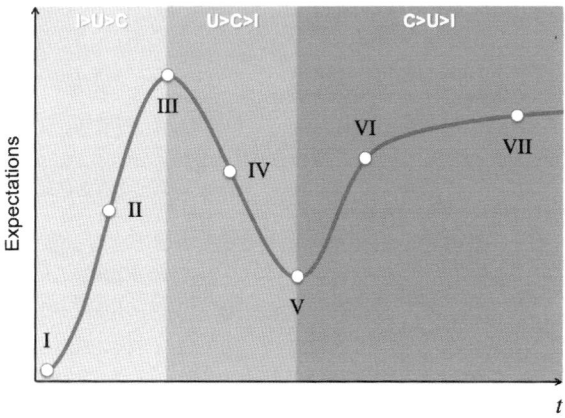

Fig. 7.1. Evolution of Evolutionary Medicine as exemplified by *Univer-city of Zurich*. (Figure adapted after "Gartner Hype cycle";[2] figure drawing by P. Eppenberger, IEM.)

Different grey phases show change in relevance at the three levels of univer-city Zurich:

I: Institute level (IEM), U: University level (UZH), C: City Level (Zurich)

Schematic milestones:

I   Initial idea and funding proposal (2010)
II Institute of Evolutionary Medicine (IEM) founded (2014)
III Total of three professorships at IEM established (2019)
IV IEM as novel yet still disruptive part of UZH recognised (+/- present)
V   IEM fully recognised as an established part of UZH (c. 2–3 years from now)

VI Evolutionary Medicine is recognised as a strategic part of the univer-city (c. several years from now)

VII Evolutionary Medicine becomes an established part of univer-city operations (c. a decade from now)

Evolutionary Medicine Perspectives at the City Level

Globally cities show — unlike countries of different sizes and economic status — often quite similar challenges. The more academic-oriented a city is, the more it is interconnected with the standing of its main universities. This interconnection is highly visible if one looks at the appeal of international conferences. In the example of Zurich Evolutionary Medicine, two international conferences, run in 2015 and 2019, showed the high level of attractiveness of both, the City of Zurich and its university as a host venue. Furthermore, the Zurich Institute of Evolutionary Medicine and its members exercise a strong public outreach. More and more media reports cover this novel field of research and teaching, and public lectures such as at the Seniors University, Community College or Children's University are in demand.

Founded in 1833, the University of Zurich was Europe's first university to be established by a democratic political system. Even nowadays there is a high dependency of this academic institution on annual budgets being approved by the very local cantonal legislative body. Thus, public outreach of researchers is of utmost importance. Local politicians decide on the University budgets most likely based on public awareness of excellence and efficiency of the University's performance when allocating taxpayer's money rather than on formal yet — as shown above — debatable assessments such as international rankings.

Although the univer-city of Zurich is not located in the federal Swiss Capital which is Bern, it has often been on the forefront of new ideas, movements or even translational innovations. Examples include Zurich being the founding centre of the "Dadaism" cultural movement c. 100 years ago; the reason for the coining of the word "coup" ("Züri-Putsch"; related to a deadly historic quarrel linked to a professorial appointment in 1839); and the first successful coronary angioplasty treatment at the local Medical Faculty in 1977. Now in the international community of medical and human biology researchers, the name "Zurich" is associated with innovative initiatives of Evolutionary Medicine.

To the contrary, discussions of new ideas "unapproved" by the line management are disappearing at the University of Adelaide. Thus, due to these unfortunate managerial developments, the university may play an increasingly reduced role in the life of society and the South Australian capital city. The local press has published articles calling the university a "degree factory" while local (state) government does not provide the expected support nor encouragement for the university to play a more prominent role in the city's economy. Instead, the state government concentrates on projects such as those involving the military industry and others supporting entertainment. The Australian Federal Government allocates university budgets based on some formal "parameters" (like numbers of enrolled students) that hardly encourage intellectual innovation nor allow for broader individual initiatives.[3]

Conclusions

As noted in the examples above, data on the factors influencing university ranking criteria illustrate how important human interactions and subjective assessments are from an evolutionary perspective. We have evolved through millennia to judge rather than to measure. This is particularly true in a complex social setting like academic institutions. To apply a "heads-up display" which would show the evolutionary perspective helps to better understand and govern unique constructs such as univer-cities. By extension, a profound evolutionary understanding of the human body and behaviour helps to build resilient supply chains in healthcare and deliver effective pandemic management that is currently lacking in how the COVID-19 is impacting the world economy. Finally, an understanding of the fact that technological and cultural cycles are faster than regulators helps to address some of our main societal challenges of today and the future.

The resilience of human-designed complex systems such as univer-cities is thus at the core of such holistic and sustainable thinking. A systemic approach based on an understanding of evolutionary theory as proposed by the concept of Evolutionary Medicine is the future at all levels: the institute the academic institution and ultimately the city.

Annex — COVID-19 (June 2020)

Univer-Cities in 1918–1919 and in 2019–2020

COVID-19 is not the first pandemic to hit univer-cities. People tend to forget catastrophes that occurred far back in time. In Switzerland there has been some sort of "disaster gap", due to the lack of major natural disasters for many years.[4] The gravest demographic catastrophe in modern Switzerland was the so-called Spanish Flu in 1918–1919, a crisis that had direct consequences for univer-cities. For example, based on a ruling from the Federal Council (18 July 1918), public events were banned and schools closed. At the University of Zurich several measures were taken due to that disastrous flu pandemic:[5] the semester ended two weeks earlier than planned and the interruption of teaching at the Medical Faculty was prolonged because many students and doctors were off-campus working at the hospitals. Due to the lack of fuel and light the semester was shifted from winter towards fall and the use of lecture rooms was restricted, e.g., on Saturdays there was complete shutdown. Also due to the lack of paper, the printing of dissertations was restricted. Furthermore, the attic of the main university building was used as a storage room for dried fruit and vegetables. Tragically, several (medical) students and lecturers of the University of Zurich died due to the Spanish flu. Such direct "intellectual" human losses among University employees have to be taken into account too when addressing the "overall costs" of pandemics at univer-cities. In comparison to the 1918–1919 flu some reactions in the current COVID-2 crisis at univer-cities are similar, such as ending the semester early. However, Swiss society was obviously very different then. Due to the high number of victims, the Swiss Public Health was de facto initiated after the 1918–1919 crisis. As a consequence the univer-city of Zurich today is better prepared and more resilient in times of a pandemic.

At the University of Adelaide there is no prominent memory of the 1918–1919 pandemic nor its effects. The current 2020 pandemic has been efficiently controlled, due to immediate and decisive actions of the State

Government of South Australia that introduced strict isolation and closure of state borders. The University of Adelaide in recent years has introduced largely virtual undergraduate teaching — all lectures are automatically recorded and many practical exercises are done virtually — and postgraduate work is conducted by email exchanges to a large extent. Thus no major interruption of teaching has occurred. The main impact, due to isolation policies, was felt by international students who constitute a large group in the University of Adelaide, some 20%. The majority of international students come from Asia, and they enliven the city by participating in shopping, dining and entertainment events. All this has been stopped, though the university provided virtual links for international students and in various ways has assured them of their continued participation in studies as soon as pandemic restrictions end. The return of international students to Adelaide is essential for its status as a univer-city which depends heavily on the economic input of such a large body of students. At the same time, many Australian graduates from basic courses, apprehensive of finding employment during the pandemic, are applying in larger numbers for postgraduate studies. Thus, the dynamics of university education and the interaction with the economy of the city are changing, but not declining significantly. Specifically, the Faculty of Health and Medical Sciences is undertaking a number of research and clinical initiatives related to fighting the pandemic. These enrich the research community of the city.

Per Aspera ad Astra

The unfolding of the COVID-19 pandemic — as far as we currently know or can assume about its origin and future dynamics — highlights the need for evolutionary thinking even more. The impact of this colossal disruption on univer-cities should be assessed with such evolutionary perspective. Individuals as well as academic structures will be most significantly affected due to this crisis. New societal values and novel expectations on the role of expert organisations will develop. Human behaviour during the pandemic has been triggered more by evolutionary than cultural imprints. This is reflected in how people act under stress due to the unknown, how they communicate, how they shop for groceries, etc.

True leadership in bottom-up organisations like universities is often overwhelmed by such unexpected challenging situations. One can see an example of this in how university management communicates (frequency, ratio of compassionate vs. technocratic communication, etc.). In the current situation this differs between the University of Zurich and University of Adelaide, with the latter having a more intense approach.

Nevertheless, cities with a strong academic imprint may be less vulnerable to non-rational behaviour and intuitive measures. Towards the end of the crisis and post-factum, other dynamics can be considered in the light of evolution, too. Generally, human inability to cope with quantitative functions (as seen in exponential case counts in pandemics) or with sustainability (as seen in a reluctance to plan for future uncommon scenarios) are other examples. The lack of willingness to maintain principles of individual hygiene and selfish or even unethical behaviours are other obvious examples explainable by evolutionary constraints.

Having evolutionary medicine established at the University of Zurich specifically helped to address such perspectives within the medical faculty as well as amongst the public (see, for example, the commentary in a major Swiss newspaper).[6] It resonated widely and its unorthodox character was appreciated. Unfortunately, there will surely be a next pandemic and the accompanying tragic toll. However, a global crisis of the magnitude similar to the present one can also offer hope and positive adaptations in the future. Univer-cities in particular can provide more societal leverage and increased self-reflection.

The Future of Univer-Cities

To summarise, universities are highly relevant during a crisis not only by providing academic knowledge and flexibility for fast-track research but also for reflection. As institutions, they allow experts embedded in their cities to address the socio-economic issues that will arise after a crisis. Members of univer-cities are most important because they can proactively cover research topics of previously unknown significance. Eventually, during a crisis these can become relevant. A classic example would be the current pandemic with all it facets. Both the universities as well as their host cities are heavily affected in such a crisis. Universities can help our vulnerable society to become more resilient. To be able to act as such an institution of support, they need to adhere to established traditional values such as academic freedom, long-term commitment to employees and bottom-up governance. Provision of space for free interaction and exchange of ideas is most critical. A university physically placed in a city, like both the University of Zurich as well as the University of Adelaide, helps to foster such an exchange even beyond traditional borders of academia. Close interaction between academia and the rest of the society is most relevant in times of crisis. A pandemic profoundly impacts the outlook on life of younger people: limits to travel and job opportunities change their decisions about the future. One of the results is greater reliance on continued education — an activity that is safe and familiar to school graduates and that offers practical investment into future employment. Therefore, applications for university studies are increasing significantly keeping school graduates in university cities and changing dynamics of city centres that are the focus of academic life, including all necessary services. The Australian Government understood this and announced funding for an increased number of places for university students that also means additional support to university finances. In times of crisis universities are increasingly seen as centres providing more than just direct economic advantages. They are places offering long-term safety of social structures, increasing value of lasting investments in knowledge, and providing the opportunity of innovation — all these factors may substantially reduce the severity of the current situation. Hope, in short.

Evolutionary Medicine can help to understand challenges we are facing in times of COVID-19 on multiple levels.[7] These include human behavioral issues, understanding of the co-evolution of host and pathogen, and finally even the problem of the lack of efficient action related to tackling a public health crisis. An evolutionary approach helps to understand and question ongoing economic challenges in times of a pandemic.[8] If one wants to know the frequently disregarded sunk cost, the opportunity costs and how they impact on people, it helps to have an evolutionary perspective. Also, the fact that medical research — as is conducted at both the University of Zurich and the University of Adelaide, in relation to current crises — might be inefficient calls for a novel perspective. Thus, based on our own experience at these two academic institutions, we propose that the knowledge and implementation of evolutionary medicine at univer-cities should be adopted to better tackle fundamental crises. The real dangers for univer-cities themselves are however — as showed above by the example of Evolutionary Medicine — not the disruption itself, but rather periods of stagnation.

Notes

1. F. Rühli and M. Henneberg, "Univer-city of Zurich: An Evolutionary-Medical Perspective" in Anthony SC Teo, ed., *Univer-Cities: Strategic Dilemmas of Medical Origins and Selected Modalities* (Singapore: World Scientific Publishing Company, 2018), pp. 77–84.

2. Jackie Fenn and Mark Raskino, *Mastering the Hype Cycle: How to Choose the Right Innovation at the Right Time* (Massachusetts: Harvard Business Press, 2008).

3. M. Henneberg, "Corporate universities down-under", *Oxford Magazine*, Second Week, Michaelmas Term (2006), pp. 16–17.

4. K. Staub, F. Rühli and J. Floris, "The 'Pandemic Gap' in Switzerland across the 20th Century and the Necessity of Increased Science Communication of Past Pandemic Experiences", Open Editorial in *Swiss Medical Weekly* (2020), <https://smw.ch/op-eds?tx_swablog_postdetail%5Bpost%5D=89>

5. University of Zurich, *Annual Report (April 1918-March 1919)* (Zürich: Art Institut Orell Füssli, 1919), p. 28ff.

6. F. Rühli «Vor dem Virus sind wir noch immer Jäger und Sammler», *Neue Zürcher Zeitung*, 11 March 2020 <https://www.nzz.ch/feuilleton/corona-virus-wir-sind-noch-immer-jaeger-und-sammler-ld.1544961?reduced=true>

7. M. Henneberg and F. Rühli, "COVID-19 and Evolutionary Medicine", Editorial in *Evolution, Medicine and Public Health* (in press), <https://doi.org/10.1093/emph/eoaa018>

8. M. Henneberg and F. Rühli, "Economy of medicine aggravates COVID-19 crisis" (under review).

About the Authors

Frank Rühli is Director of the Institute of Evolutionary Medicine, at the University of Zurich (UZH), Switzerland, and is member of the parliament of the City of Zurich.

Maciej Henneberg is now retired, he was the Wood Jones Professor of Anthropological and Comparative Anatomy at the University of Adelaide, Australia.

CHAPTER EIGHT

PHINMA TRANSFORMING EDUCATION: INEQUALITIES IN THE PHILIPPINES

FRANCIS L. LARIOS AND ROSEANNE AGAS RAMIREZ

"Even as a child, it has been my dream to finish my studies, rise from poverty, and help my family."

PHINMA Araullo University graduate now working in Australia

PHINMA Education, the education services subsidiary of PHINMA Corporation, focuses on the challenge of providing accessible, quality education to students from low-income backgrounds. Most of them come from families that earn about US$300 per month. Most of them are hoping to be the first in their family to finish college. However, they are most probably not prepared for college, if we look at their scores on a college-readiness test. But they aspire to have a job, like their more well-off counterparts. However their chances of getting a job usually reserved for college graduates are not as high as their counterparts. This is where we see the inequalities.

Underserved students coming from low-income families face three major challenges with regards to higher education institutions (HEIs).

The first is the challenge of access. That is, "Can I get into college?"

The second is the challenge of completion. That is, "Can I finish college?"

The third is the challenge of employability. That is, "Can I get a job after I graduate?"

Increasing Access to College

To ease the entry of underserved students into tertiary education, we ask for minimum entrance requirements. While many tertiary institutions may require entrance exams, we accept a student as long as she has a high school diploma.

We are also among the schools with the lowest tuition fees in the Philippines. The fees are US$600 per year.

A significant percentage of our student population benefits from the Handog Kaibigan (Friendship Grant) scholarship programme, or HK. The programme offers effectively a 40% scholarship to qualified students, based on their Poverty Probability Index (PPI) scores. It is unlike scholarship programmes offered by other private HEIs because of the breadth of its coverage — one for every three college students in PHINMA schools enjoys this privilege.

The subsidy provided by the HK and the low tuition fees open up opportunities for many low-income students to obtain tertiary education at PHINMA schools.

What helps us keep tuition fees affordable?

PHINMA Education has various cost-effectiveness initiatives that contribute to the decreasing cost per student, and thus keeps tuition fees affordable.

Nevertheless, we maintain a high teacher-student ratio and the required minimum number of teachers with a doctorate degree.

The use of lean administrative teams and a consolidated backroom allows PHINMA Education to keep its labour overhead costs low. Key decisions in finance, human resources, marketing, and operations are made at the level of the Head Office. This model leverages the expertise of top talent and maximises their capability to oversee programmes at the school level. Individual schools have programme implementers who are accountable to just one department head. Thus, the cost of key decision-makers is shared among the schools.

We also conduct the minimum amount of research required by the Ministry of Education.

Energy-saving equipment, LED lights, solar power, and water recycling is used across all schools. PHINMA Solar is a trusted partner in providing solar power. Rainwater catchment facilities and greywater reuse in schools have drastically reduced spending on water. Further, regular energy audits are conducted by responsibility centres in schools.

The general principle is that if something does not help move the needle in terms of access, completion, or employability, we most likely will not spend on it. This principle has enabled us to offer the HK scholarship to 33% of our college students. It has also enabled us to pay our teachers well.

Helping Students Finish College

In addition to keeping tuition fees affordable, other initiatives help our students finish college.

College Completion Assistance Program

We provide our students with a US$600 benefit if the person supporting their education passes away, falls sick, or loses his/her job. It functions like a tuition fee insurance that lessens the shock of a family financial emergency. The premium is US$7, paid by all students per semester. Last year, we serviced nineteen claims.

Student Success Program

The Student Success Program (SSP) is a co-curricular programme required for all students. It is based on the three principles of (1) I want, (2) I can, and (3) I belong.

- *I Want.* The first principle helps students identify a vision of a fulfilling life and how to use education to achieve concrete goals. Its end goal is to provide them with the motivation to do their best despite difficulties.
- *I Can.* The second principle is about showing students that intelligence is malleable and anything can be learned through a combination of trying, practicing, receiving feedback, learning from the experience.
- *I Belong.* The third principle emphasises that students just like them have succeeded before — and so they can, too. It shows them that they are a part of a supportive community; as they receive and then, later on, give support to others just like them.

Aside from the modules that develop these principles, the programme also utilises Monitoring and Mentoring sessions to conduct proactive advising to help students deal with everything from academic to personal challenges.

SSP helps students graduate on time with the skills and mindsets necessary to succeed in work and life because students know what they WANT, know that they CAN achieve their goals, and know that they BELONG in a PHINMA Education school.

Active Learning

How do we scale up effective and engaging teaching that helps our students learn despite having a weak foundation in basic education? The Great Teacher Program (GTP) is our way for our teachers to develop the proficiency of teaching in an Active Learning (AL) way. It features an AL crash course, an AL toolkit with suggested teaching strategies and resource links, additional training modules, and a coaching programme.

Other Retention Efforts

Beyond this, Students-at-Risk (StaRs) are carefully monitored to reduce dropout rates. Advisers and school management regularly communicate with them. When necessary, a team is dispatched to their homes to seek feedback from students and parents on their situation. Interventions in the form of financial or emotional support are always offered.

Helping Students Secure a Job

Involving industry in curriculum development and training allows PHINMA Education to ensure its programmes are relevant and its graduates are work-ready. The company fosters a good relationship with numerous industry partners that provide certificates, seminars, internships, and valuable input in curriculum design.

One such partner, the School D'Hospitality (SDH) Institute in Singapore, makes it possible for our Hospitality, Tourism, and Business Administration students to earn an internationally-recognised diploma on top of their bachelor's degree at the end of their four-year course. With the additional modules from SDH, qualified students have the chance to equip themselves with a wide range of practical and industry-grounded skills that will give them an edge over other regular graduates.

Another programme that helps in the employability of our students is the Success Ladder. It is an approach borne out of the reality that the majority of low-income students entering tertiary education will not be able to graduate. It is a framework that helps our students gain employable skills every semester or every year. Thus, even if a student leaves a programme midstream, the student is more employable than prior to starting the course.

Results

Due in large part to our teachers' efforts to focus on effective and engaging learning, graduates' performance in various licensure examinations has improved significantly. In the last five years, the average overall passing rate (ratio of total passers to total takers) is 74%, in contrast to an average of 56% in the previous six to ten years. Since starting operations, PHINMA Education has produced over 20,000 licensed professionals (about 7,000 of them in the past five years).

Most graduates of PHINMA Education are employed within one year from graduation. Internal graduate tracer studies conducted from 2014 to 2018, showed that over 80% of the graduates are employed within one year from graduation, with more than half of them finding their first job within the first three months from graduation.

Broadening Our Mission

Ultimately, PHINMA Education's unique value proposition is to help students, who face inequalities in access, completion, and employability, secure their first job without paying for an expensive college education. We pay close attention to the needs and aspirations of our market. We ensure that they are supported not only financially but also emotionally and mentally as well. We strive so that our mission of making lives better through education is reflected in every policy and intervention in each of our schools in the Philippines.

From 5,000 students in a lone school in Central Luzon when it started operations in 2004, PHINMA Education has grown into a network of 74,000 students and six institutions in 15 years. This translates to a compounded annual enrolment growth of 18.6% or 7.10% organic growth (excluding new acquisitions) yearly. College freshman enrolment has more than doubled from eight years ago (i.e., from about 8,000 in SY 2011–2012, to about 22,000 in SY 2019–2020). And our mission has taken us beyond the Philippines to a new school in Indonesia.

The main motivation of the company to expand outside the Philippines is the recognition that there is a large underserved market among low income youth aspiring to higher education in the ASEAN. Indonesia's tertiary gross enrolment ratio is 36% and its population totals 267 million. PHINMA Education's business and academic model is designed primarily to cater to the needs, challenges and aspirations of this segment and it is this technology that the company brings in its joint venture partnerships outside the Philippines. Thus, through a joint venture agreement with Indonesian group Tripersada Global Manajemen, PHINMA Education formed PT Ind Phil Management (IPM) to manage STIKES and STMIK Kharisma Karawang in West Java.

Throughout the years and across locations, PHINMA Education has remained committed to contributing to the world's efforts of removing inequalities in education and employability. By continuously learning and improving its own way of doing things, it hopes to positively impact more youth in the Philippines and in Southeast Asia, towards a future that is sustainable for all.

About **PHINMA** Education

PHINMA Education Holdings Inc., under the conglomerate PHINMA Corporation, started investing in the education services sector in 2004 through the acquisition of Araullo University in Nueva Ecija. It has since expanded its presence across the country with its network of schools including Cagayan de Oro College in Misamis Oriental, University of Pangasinan in Pangasinan, University of Iloilo in Iloilo City, Southwestern University in Cebu City, Saint Jude College in Manila, Republican College in Quezon City, and Rizal College of Laguna. It has also expanded overseas with PHINMA Education PT Ind Phil Management in Indonesia.

In August 2019, PHINMA Education was shortlisted in the FT/IFC Transformational Business Awards' education category. The awards, open to 278 organisations with programmes in 126 countries, recognise, showcase, and reward private sector innovation, impact, replicability, financial viability and sustainability across key areas identified in the UN Sustainable Development Goals (SDGs).

About the Authors

Francis L. Larios is the Chief Learning Officer of PHINMA Education. Francis holds a Bachelor of Arts in Social Sciences from Ateneo de Manila University. His team co-designs and improves programmes that help their students get into school, finish school, and secure a job, whether they finish their schooling or not.

Roseanne Agas Ramirez is a writer and educator who joined PHINMA Education in 2019 as a Corporate Communications Specialist. She holds a Bachelor of Arts in Political Science and a Master of Asian Studies from the University of the Philippines Diliman.

CHAPTER NINE

PROVIDING CLEAN AND SAFE WATER TO ALL: A GLOBAL PERSPECTIVE

ASIT K. BISWAS AND CECILIA TORTAJADA

Introduction

Neither human beings nor ecosystems can survive without water. Not surprisingly, the British-American poet, W. H. Auden, wrote: "Thousands have lived without love, but none without water."

While the importance of water for human and ecosystem survival has been known for thousands of years, water has not been on the international political agenda until around the mid-1970s. In 1977, during the United Nations Water Conference, held at a very high decision-making level, it firmly entered the global political agenda for the first time. This Conference declared the decade of 1981–1990 to be the International Drinking Water Supply and Sanitation Decade (IDWSSD). This was approved by the United Nations General Assembly. The objective was that by the end of this Decade, every person in the world would have access to clean water and adequate sanitation (Biswas, 1978). The target was very ambitious, and, not surprisingly, it could not be met. However, by any definition, the Decade was remarkably successful since it ensured that hundreds of millions of people in the developing world had access to water which would not have happened without the forces that were unleashed by this Decade (Biswas and Tortajada, 2009).

Nearly three decades later, in July 2010, the United Nations General Assembly declared water to be a human right (UN, 2010). This gave another impetus towards reaching universal access to clean and safe water.

At present, a decade after the United Nations Generally Assembly declared water to be a human right, the global situation with respect to the availability of clean water has become even more complex and somewhat more convoluted than ever before. During the 1980-2017 period, an objective analysis will indicate that the focus of the world was primarily on providing water to the people, and make access to it easier. As long as the people had access to water, it was assumed that this was all that was needed. During this period, led by two major UN agencies, WHO and UNICEF, and followed by all international and national organisations, a meaningless term "improved sources of water" was devised. Unfortunately, it has absolutely no relation, or linkage, to water quality. By comprehensively fudging the water quality issue for over nearly four decades, the entire United Nations System was able to claim, erroneously, in 2012, that the Millennium Development Goal (MDG) target on water was achieved three years ahead of the deadline of 2015 (WHO/UNICEF, 2012). In reality, this was incorrect. There is no question that more people had better access to water than ever before in history. However, overall, the quality of water they received was dubious. In the entire developing world, very few people believed that the water supplied was either clean or safe to drink.

Water Quality and Health

Irrespective of the claims of the various United Nations agencies and international organisations, the fact still remains that the clean water and the sanitation targets of the Millennium Development Goals in the areas of water supply and sanitation were not met by 2015. In fact, in nearly all urban areas of developing countries, the quality of water in rivers, lakes and aquifers has steadily deteriorated over time. This is because of ineffective and inadequate management of wastewater from domestic and industrial sources. Since the varied qualities of the water sources deteriorated steadily and utilities did not treat, or were incapable of treating water adequately, households in developing countries did not perceive that the piped water they received in their houses was safe to drink without any health concerns.

In developing countries, even in 2020, significant percentages of domestic wastewater are still not being collected and then taken to wastewater treatment plants for any proper treatment. Industrial wastewater faces very similar problems. Domestic wastewaters at least are biodegradable over time. In contrast, industrial wastewaters may contain hundreds of conservative contaminants, like chemicals, heavy metals and other hazardous materials, that do not break down over time. In addition, agricultural run-off containing chemicals like pesticides and fertilisers, further contaminate both surface and groundwaters by leaching. At present, only about 10-12% of the people in the developing world have access to proper wastewater collection, treatment and disposal. In the absence of proper domestic and industrial wastewater collection and adequate treatments, water quality all over the developing world has undergone continuous deterioration over the past five decades. This trend, most regrettably, is still continuing in much of the developed world.

Decades of neglect of proper domestic, industrial and agricultural wastewater management have ensured that all water bodies around and within population centres of the developing world are now seriously contaminated with numerous known and unknown pollutants. Equally, most urban water utilities in developing countries currently do not have adequate capacities, technological, management and administrative expertise, nor the funds to treat bulk raw water properly before supplying to households. Thus, the trust and the confidence of the people in the quality of water they receive from their utilities have progressively deteriorated, and currently, for all practical purposes, are almost non-existent.

In addition, as the levels of income and literacy have progressively increased in all developing countries, people have become increasingly aware of the potential adverse health implications of using not properly treated piped water.

The public awareness of the interlinkages between the quality of water and human health has been further heightened by the communication and information revolution that has been witnessed in all developing countries over the past 30 years. Wide availability of mobile phones, 24-hours news channels, and a wide range of television channels, including independent ones, in nearly all developing countries have contributed to the growing awareness of the potential adverse health impacts of using not properly treated water. In fact, in nearly all South Asian countries, significantly more people currently have mobile phones than toilets! Mobile phones have become a source of information even for illiterate or semi-literate people. Thus, the knowledge base of nearly all the people, rich or poor, literate or illiterate, has increased dramatically in recent decades. Currently, nearly every person is aware of the interlinkages between unclean water and health in some fashion. They have also become aware that the quality of water that is being supplied by their utilities leaves much to be desired, and thus is somewhat dangerous to drink, in terms of health, without additional treatments in their individual homes.

Water Quality in Developing Countries

Over the past several decades, most households in the cities of developing countries have progressively transformed themselves into mini-utilities to cope adequately with both intermittent piped water supply and poor water quality.

Water supply in the majority of the urban centres is now intermittent. Often, households receive two hours of water in the mornings, one hour around noon, and another one to two hours during the evenings. Actual number of hours when they receive water is around three to five hours each day. This intermittent pattern of water supply is the norm rather than exception in most cities of developing countries of Africa, Asia or Latin America. During drought years, even this intermittent water supply is further reduced.

Most households, from India to Egypt, and Jordan to Mexico, have transformed this intermittent water supply to a continuous 24x7 flow by constructing their own mini-utility which has been, for the most part, quite effective. Households have constructed underground tanks where water is stored whenever there is supply. This is complemented by the construction of smaller overhead tanks. The two tanks are then connected by a pipe and a pumping system which pumps water from the underground tank to the overhead tank as and when needed. From the overhead tank water flows to individual houses or apartments by gravity, whenever needed, during day or night.

Each household thereafter purifies their own water for drinking and cooking, or they buy 20L jugs sold commercially. Some two to three decades ago, households used carbon filters to treat their own water supply. As technology has developed, economic conditions have improved, and the economy of scale has reduced prices of treatment processes significantly, the preferred mode of cleaning has increasingly become reverse osmosis (RO). However, the RO system used in households is not efficient: about 60-70% of total water processed currently ends up as wastewater, and then mostly is thrown away.

In terms of continuous water availability, the coping strategy currently used has been generally quite effective. However, in terms of improving water quality by installing in-house water treatment processes, the results have been varied, depending upon the operation and maintenance practices of individual households.

This is because to maintain reasonably good water quality, membranes for reverse osmosis, or filters for the filtration systems, have to be changed as and when necessary. The timing of this change will depend primarily upon the quantities and qualities of water treated. Unfortunately, most households do not change membranes or filters as frequently warranted, often because of lack of knowledge, or to save money, or pure lethargy. An overwhelming number of households change the filters or membranes at regular intervals, say between every three to six months. Thus, the systems do not operate efficiently when membranes or filters are not fully functional. This means that the quality of water each household drinks could still be dubious after treatments.

Another major problem stems from the fact that all households must clean their underground and overhead tanks regularly, say every two to three months which is not always the case. These two tanks are major sources of contamination, unless they are cleaned properly and regularly. Accordingly, the bacteriological qualities of water in these tanks deteriorate over time. If membranes or filters are not efficient in removing pollutants, then the quality of water people drink is not safe, and thus could pose serious health hazards.

Regrettably, most households are not aware of the importance of these issues in terms of health implications. Water utilities do not consider it their task to make households aware of these requirements since the equipment belongs to individual households and not to the utilities. Thus, households often are not getting clean and safe water all the time, even after spending significant personal funds to improve the quality of piped water.

Water Quality in Developed Countries

A myth has developed over several decades that proper domestic water supply is an issue only for developing countries, and that the developed countries mostly solved their water problems over half-century ago. Very few academics have seriously and objectively analysed the overall status of water quality in developed countries. In this chapter, we cover the serious problems that some developed countries have been facing on the quality of water they receive from their utilities.

Loss of confidence and trust in the quality of piped water in developing countries should not come as a surprise to most people. It has been there for decades. What is most surprising is that the people in developed countries have started to lose trust and confidence in the quality of water they are receiving from their utilities for a variety of reasons. This loss of trust and confidence has increased steadily during the past two decades.

Water quality in urban centres of developed countries is presenting different types of problems compared to those experienced in developing countries. During the 1960s, 1970s and 1980s, and even in 1990s, an overwhelming majority of households in these countries used to drink water straight from the tap, without any health concerns. During these decades, very few households had in-house water treatment systems. Further, the use of bottled water was very limited, mostly under certain very special conditions.

During the 1990s, this situation started to change for several reasons. Starting from the early 1990s, several water utilities of important Western cities had poor management practices which resulted in serious and well-publicised health crises, including deaths of consumers. These incidents forced people to ponder on how good is the overall quality of water that they were receiving from the utilities. Also, if this water was safe enough for them and their family members to drink straight from the tap without any potential adverse health implications.

Consider the United States, the world's only superpower. Economically and technologically, it is the most important country of the globe. Yet, between 1982 and 2015, in any specific year, between 9 to 45 million Americans received drinking water from their utilities that violated the country's Safe Drinking Water Act. These violations have generally continued to increase during this period. However, except for some major well-known failures in important urban centres, most of the people at risk live in rural and low-income areas (Allaire, Wu and Lall, 2018).

Many widely publicised failures of water utilities in the United States and Canada have steadily eroded confidence and trust in the quality of water from the utilities. These failures have contributed to serious unease of the population in other developed countries with regard to the quality of water they are receiving. An implicit assumption has been that if such catastrophic failures can occur in the most economically advanced country of the world, like the United States, can the water supply in their countries, which is less advanced than the US, be safe?

Among these serious failures have been the following. In 1993, in the city of Milwaukee, US, 403,000 persons, that is, one quarter of its population, became sick when the filtration system of one of the two water treatment plants failed to remove *Cryptosporidium oocysts* effectively. This resulted in substantial medical costs and productivity losses of the affected households, estimated at $96.3 million (Corso *et al.*, 2003).

In May 2000, the worst Canadian public health disaster involving a water utility occurred in Walkerton, Ontario. The water supply system was contaminated by deadly strains of *Escherichia coli* and *Campylobacter jejuni* bacteria. At least seven people died and more than 2,300 people became seriously ill. This tragedy occurred due to improper operation and maintenance of the municipal water supply system and the decisions of the Ontario Government to cut staff and budgets in order to transfer the infrastructure responsibilities from the province to the municipality (Hipel, Zhao and Kilgour, 2003).

Probably the event that greatly shook the confidence of people in the Western world took place in Flint, Michigan, US. The city's source of water used to be from Lake Huron. However, to ensure sufficient amount of water is available for a growing population, the city decided to change its source of bulk water from the Lake Huron to the Flint River, in April 2014. This changeover was very poorly planned and carried out without serious considerations of the quality of source water and what impacts this could have on the network and the health of its inhabitants. The impacts of the change were soon noticed by the residents. Within a few weeks of the switch, residents started to complain about colour, taste and odour of the piped water. During the summer of 2014, E. Coli and total coliform violations meant three boil-water alerts had to be issued within a 22-day period. This should not have come as a surprise since at the time of the switch, water quality of the Flint River was very poor due to decades of poor water quality management, including regular discharges of unregulated wastewater from domestic and industrial sources.

The problem was further compounded because the city officials failed to ensure that proper corrosion control measures were added to the new sources of water which was significantly more acidic, and thus more corrosive, than the earlier source from the Lake Huron. This corrosion contributed to intensified lead leaching from old lead pipes to the drinking water supply that was being received by the Flint residents.

During the summers of 2014 and 2015, 91 cases of legionellosis were also observed in Flint, with nine deaths. These levels were much higher than what was witnessed earlier.

The Flint public officials claimed for years that no link could be proven between the health hazards suffered by the Flint residents and the switch in water supply. Accordingly, they erroneously argued that the new water source was not to be blamed. However, several independent studies as well as one by the US Environmental Protection Agency (EPA) confirmed dangerous levels of lead in water in the city, and also high levels of lead in the blood of children.

Eventually, President Barack Obama declared a federal emergency in Flint on 16 January 2016 (Obama White House, 2016). This released up to $5 million of Federal aid to immediately assist with the public health crisis. It authorised Federal Emergency Management Agency (FEMA) to cover 75% of the costs of providing bottled water, filters, filter cartridges, etc., to the Flint residents. The balance of 25% was covered by the Michigan State.

Flint has now become a global cause célèbre for gross mismanagement of a water utility. It resulted in extensive coverage in the world media, in both developed and developing countries, as well as in a popular film and well over 15 books. Former Republican Governor of Michigan, Rick Snyder, admitted at a Congressional hearing, in 2016, that the Flint water crisis "was a failure of government at all levels. Local, state and federal officials — we all failed the families of Flint" (Committee on Oversight and Reform, 2016). The general assumption of most people in the developed world has often been if such mismanagement of water utility can happen in the world's richest and technologically most advanced country, this could happen anywhere, including in their hometown.

The global publicity on Flint was not limited merely to two to four years. It has become an ongoing saga that is likely to contribute to further the reduction of public trust and confidence in the quality of water the people receive from their water utilities, irrespective of whether they live in developed or developing countries.

This adverse publicity will continue for several more years to come. In August 2020, the State of Michigan reached a settlement to pay $600 million to the victims of the Flint debacle. This generated further publicity and brought further public attention to the Flint fiasco.

Flint will continue to remain in the public eye for many more years to come. The State has now settled with the people of Flint. Felony charges that were initially filed against more than half a dozen state officials were dismissed in 2019. However, criminal investigations by the Attorney General's Department of Michigan are now ongoing for possible legal actions. Legal fallouts from the Flint crisis will thus continue for several years to come. This will result in further adverse publicity for water utilities all around the world.

Unfortunately, Flint's water crisis was not an isolated incident. Soon its echoes were felt in other parts of the United States. A somewhat similar event occurred in 2016, in Newark and northern New Jersey. Elevated levels of lead in water were observed in many public schools throughout the city. In 2017, more than 22% of drinking water samples tested had higher lead levels than stipulated by the federal standards. The reason for high lead content in piped water was very similar to that of Flint: failure of proper corrosion control treatment programme for an acidic water source. An estimated 18,000 homes in Newark had lead pipes which connected the households to the water mains. Lead leached from these pipes and reached the domestic consumers.

It should be noted that lead pipes were quite popular in the United States up to around the 1980s. Compared to iron pipes, they were more flexible and durable, and thus were preferred. The US Environmental Protection Agency started regulating lead from June 1991 when it published a regulation known as the *Lead and Copper Rule* (USEPA, 1991).

This Rule established an action level for lead at 15 parts per billion (0.015mg/L) and for copper at 1.3 parts per million (1.3 mg/L). There is considerable medical consensus at present that no level of lead is safe. All the European Union countries and Canada are now limiting lead levels to 5 ppb, that is 1/3rd of the permissible levels in the US. Permissible copper levels in European Union countries, at 1.00 ppm, are also less than the US, but not as much as for lead.

A major problem in the United States is its community water utilities are highly fragmented. There are over 50,000 water utilities. Many of them are small and thus do not have the resources or capacity to monitor water quality to determine if they comply with the EPA regulations not only for lead but also for all other contaminants, let alone to take proper and timely corrective measures when warranted. Not surprisingly, more than 20% of the water utilities do not know if they have lead service lines to households within the area they serve (Cornwell, Brown and Via, 2016). Nearly 30% of the water utilities have reported the presence of lead service lines.

A survey has estimated that the country has at least 6.1 million lead service lines which serve around 15-20 million people by community water systems (AWWA Engineering Modeling Applications Committee, 2020). They have either full or partial lead service lines serving households. This represents nearly 7% of the people served by such water systems. The number of lead service lines is estimated at between 6.1 to 11 million, which would represent around 50,000 miles of lead service lines. These means that, between 1 January 2015 and 31 March 2018, nearly 5.5 million Americans received water that exceeded EPA's lead action level. There were 13,991 violations of the EPA's *Lead and Copper Rule* by 8,339 community water systems during this period.

Replacing all the lead pipelines is likely to cost over $30 billion. Unfortunately, not only in the United States but also in nearly all developed countries, with very few exceptions like Singapore, there have been gross under-investments in the domestic water supply sector for generations. Singapore is probably the only developed country which uses the concept of preventive maintenance. For example, for several decades, it has been replacing about 2% of its total water networks. This means the whole network is renewed every 50 years. In recent years, Singapore has been using sensors to determine the weakest links in their network and then replacing them.

In much of the Western world, water pipes were laid more than 50 to 100 years ago. In some parts of the US, some pipelines even date back to the time of the Civil War of the 1860s. Many of these are lead pipes. Equally, there are several water supply treatment plants in the US which are using pre-World War I treatment technologies. In contrast, Singapore uses the latest technologies and management practices to treat its bulk raw water and wastewater (Tortajada, Joshi and Biswas, 2013).

The American Society of Civil Engineers (ASCE) has been producing an Infrastructure Report Card every four years, for various sectors, since 2001. The grade A is considered to be exceptional, fit for the future; B is good, adequate for now; C is for mediocre, requires attention; and the lowest is D for poor, at risk. Between 2001 and 2017, drinking water infrastructure had consistently received either the grade of D or D⁻ from ASCE. In 2017, this sector received a grade D. The 2017 report noted that there were an estimated 240,000 water main breaks each year, resulting in loss of over two trillion gallons of treated water (ASCE, 2017). Overall, some six billion gallons of treated water are lost annually due to leaks. An estimated $1 trillion is needed to maintain and expand service to meet the demands properly and efficiently for the next 25 years.

The neglect of America's drinking water infrastructure, like all other types of infrastructure, ranging from airports to highways, has been well documented for several years. However, the political system has never seen the urgency and importance of providing adequate financing to improve them.

The validity of the grade D, given by ASCE to the American drinking water infrastructure is confirmed by the American Water Works Association (AWWA). Each year AWWA publishes a report on the state of the water industry. This report is an industry-wide self-assessment of the latest status of the sector. In its latest report (AWWA, 2019), it noted that the biggest and most critical challenge being faced by this sector was renewal and replacement of water and wastewater infrastructure. This can only be accomplished by combined and determined efforts of all three levels of the government — Federal, State and Municipal — to have adequate financing in place over the long term. This, regrettably, has not happened over generations, and thus the cumulative costs of fixing them have increased steadily over the decades. The total costs of updating and fixing America's poor infrastructure have now become astronomical.

With the current budget deficit running at about 20% of GDP in the United States, the chances of American Congress and all individual States earmarking substantial sums, on a long-term basis, for updating and improving drinking water infrastructure systematically and continuously are very slim.

Thus, the most likely scenario is likely to be there will be actions and funding availability, on an ad hoc basis, only when major crises occur, such as at Flint or Newark, and when there is considerable public and media scrutiny as well as serious and sustained pressures on all the three levels of the government to act quickly.

America is not only facing serious water quality problems of serious contaminations due to hazardous contaminants but also from non-point sources of pollution due to its large scale agricultural and animal hus-bandry farms. Proper water quality management due to large scale dis-posal of animal waste has been a serious problem not only in the United States but also in the rest of the world.

Large industrial scale cattle and hog farming produces enormous amount of animal waste. Agricultural farms use fertilisers extensively, including spreading manure, much of which leaches into groundwater and rivers. They contaminate all water sources. In rural America, numerous households depend on private wells for domestic water supply. It is esti-mated that 43 million people depend on them as their primary water source. A sample survey by the United States Geological Survey indicated that around 20% of these wells are contaminated (USGS, 2009).

A state report on water quality of private wells for Wisconsin noted that nearly 6% of its nearly 676,000 private wells exceeded the federal health standards for nitrates. In 2018, 40% of surface water samples tested in Nebraska had nitrate levels above EPA's safe limit of 10 ppm for drinking water. This limit was set in 1962 because of infant methemo-globinemia where babies skin turns blue because of decreased amount of haemoglobin in the blood. This could result in fatalities.

In 2020, at least four billion people in both developed and developing countries do not trust the quality of water they receive from the tap.

In the US, at least two million people do not have access to piped water and basic sanitary facilities. The indigenous people of Australia, Canada and the United States currently receive water which is of poorer quality than received by the residents of a third world city like Phnom Penh in Cambodia (Biswas, Sachdeva and Tortajada, 2021).

European Initiatives

Unlike the United States and Canada, the European Parliament approved plans on 23 October 2018 to increase the confidence of its citizens on the quality of the water they receive from their utilities. Concurrently, they took steps to promote the use of tap water in all the EU countries, and to ensure that all its inhabitants are provided with better, reliable and regular information on the water they receive. Tap water is safe and reliable in all the EU countries (European Parliament, 2018*a*).

The EU Parliament also took steps to reduce the use of single use plastic bottles for drinking water so that EU citizens can lower their use of plastics. Plastic water bottles are the most found single use plastic item on the EU beaches. This step would also contribute to reduction of litter found in the oceans. According to the estimates of the European Commission, reducing the use of water consumption from these plastic bottles could save the EU citizens more than 600 million Euros each year (European Parliament, 2019).

The legislation also reduces the allowable permissible level of lead by half as well as a further reduction in bacterial content of drinking water. It has, for the first time, introduced caps for certain endocrine disruptors, and requires monitoring of microplastics in all drinking water supplies. All these measures were taken not only to improve further the quality of water that all EU citizens receive but also to ensure that their trust and confidence in tap water would improve significantly. These steps were aimed at increasing the use of tap water and concurrently reducing the extent of use of bottled water.

The legislation further asks all member states to ensure universal access to clean water, especially for the marginalised and the vulnerable groups. It also encourages the EU states to set up free water fountains in public places where necessary and technically feasible. The countries should also encourage restaurants, canteens and catering services to provide tap water, either free or for a low service charge.

On 18 December 2019, both the EU Parliament and the EU Council reached a provisional agreement to modify the existing EU Drinking Water Directive (European Parliament, 2018*b*). It added an upper limit for an endocrine disruptor, Bisphenol A, at 2.5 parts per billion. Two other endocrine disruptors, Beta-estradiol and Nonylphenol, will be included in its first watch list. The new Directive is expected to enter into force sometime during the summer of 2020.

With this new modified directive, the regulations to ensure good quality of drinking water in the EU countries will become one of the most stringent in the world.

Changing Global Perceptions, Trust and Confidence on Water Quality Following COVID-19

As discussed earlier, the management of drinking water quality in both developed and developing countries has left much to be desired during the past several decades. The issues related to drinking water quality and people's trust and confidence in it have become even more complex since December 2019, with the emergence of COVID-19. This new coronavirus, which jumped from animals to humans, has played havoc with human health and well-being.

The pandemic has created global crises not only in terms of health but also in financial, industrial, employment, social, and many other sectors, including food, water and transportation.

For the water sector, its impacts have been many, some known but others are still amorphous and not yet evident. What is certain is that COVID-19 will have many short, medium and long-term impacts on water quality. The extent, magnitude and duration of these impacts are likely to vary from country to country, depending upon how effective their efforts will be to manage the coronavirus pandemic, people's trust, confidence and reactions to government policies and actions, and a whole range of other factors, some known but others unknown and unpredictable.

From the perspective of the domestic water supply and wastewater management, COVID-19 has already made serious impacts on the people's and the policy-makers' perceptions and actions on water quality. People all over the world, for the first time, understood and realised the importance of frequent and proper handwashing with clean water and soap, and practice of good personal hygiene habits. In nearly all countries, people propelled by fear and uncertainties, for the first time, learnt how to wash hands properly with soap and clean water at frequent intervals. Earlier studies in many countries have indicated that most people, in both developed and developing countries, were not washing their hands properly or regularly. As a result, in reality, many of the germs were removed not by handwashing but during the process of wiping hands with paper or cloth towels. This is also one reason why coliform bacteria is widely present in the mobile phones of a significant percentage of the people, in both developed and developing countries. COVID-19 has changed the behaviour of the people, including their handwashing habits, at least over the near- and medium-term.

COVID-19 also has radically changed, positively, people's attitudes and perceptions of clean water and its importance and indispensability to maintain their health and also that of their families. The fear generated by COVID-19, for the first time, has forced a significant percentage of people all over the world to wash hands both properly and frequently, and to realise the critical necessity of having access to clean and safe water to maintain their health and well-being.

Unfortunately, up to now, water quality issues have received mostly cursory interest from policy-makers of most developing and developed countries. There has been considerable political rhetoric on the importance of access to clean water. However, actual and realistic implementable policies have often been conspicuous by their absence in nearly all developing countries and, to a certain extent, in many developed countries as well.

Further, sustainability of rules and regulations, and their strict enforcements, on a long-term basis, has been a serious constraint for many countries.

If one considers a highly developed country like the United States, one of its most successful policies has been the Clean Water Act. This was approved by the Congress in 1972, and then strengthened several times over the past four decades or so. The Act has been instrumental in regulating and maintaining quality standards for surface waters. This Act, by all accounts, has been very successful in improving the quality of water that the American households have received over recent decades. However, the latest US Administration has started to chip away many of the restrictions that were imposed to maintain the quality of America's water bodies. This does not bode well for either the American people or the environment over the medium- and long-term.

In contrast to the US, the countries of the European Union, Singapore and China have been progressively tightening water quality rules and regulations to ensure the quality of water that their population receives continues to remain safe. The EU countries are somewhat advanced in this area. For example, they are among the very few countries that have imposed an upper permissible level on the presence of a known endocrine disruptor, as mentioned earlier, and monitor other such potential disruptors and as well as microplastics in drinking water.

Similarly, since 2019 Singapore has been monitoring 346 water quality parameters. As more and more pollutants are considered to be important, PUB, Singapore's National Water Agency, monitors them regularly. Figure 9.1 shows how the number of water quality parameters being monitored by Singapore has gone up very significantly during the 1963–2019 period. In 1963, PUB was monitoring 35 parameters. This number has increased to 346. This means the number of water quality parameters PUB is monitoring has

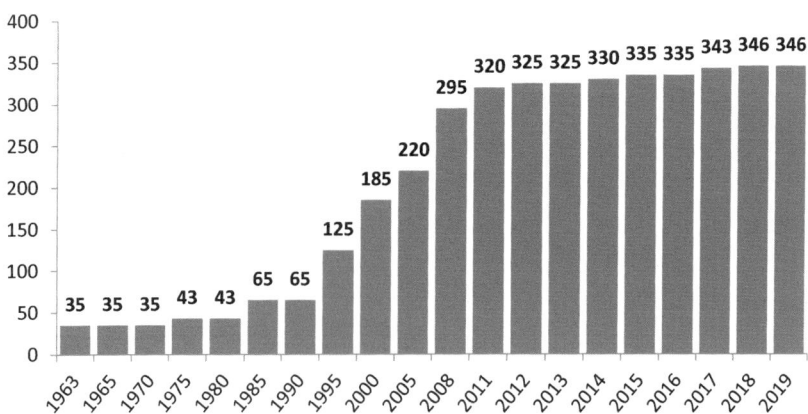

Fig. 9.1. Number of water quality parameters monitored by the PUB in Singapore, 1963-2019.

Source: Public Utilities Board, Singapore.

increased nearly 10-fold during the past 56 years. The city-state also imposes significantly stricter rules and regulations, increasing penalties to industry for violating the norms, very strict enforcement of all laws, regulations, and institutional restructuring as and when necessary. This has significantly changed the water quality management landscape in Singapore. On the basis of trends of the last five years, one can predict fairly safely that the quality of its water sources is likely to further improve appreciably by 2030.

In the case of China, the country has been giving significantly greater attention in recent years to manage water quality. In order to ensure that Chinese households are receiving good quality water, the country recently nearly trebled the number of water quality parameters to over 110 that must be measured regularly. This is in sharp contrast to another major developing country, India. Indian utilities currently measure mostly 15–30 water quality parameters. This unfortunate situation, especially after the massive infections and deaths due to COVID-19, will most certainly further aggravate even the very limited trust and confidence in the quality of water that the Indians receive at present. This is likely to encourage most Indian households to see what they can do by their efforts to further improve the quality of water they are receiving from the utilities.

Meeting Sustainable Development Goals in Developing Countries

Even before the COVID-19 struck the world, progress in meeting various SDGs had slowed down perceptibly. For example, for the water and sanitation sectors, overseas development assistance (ODA) increased by 38% during 2016 and 2017. In 2018, ODA declined by 9% compared to 2017 (UN, 2020). After the unexpected massive expenditures in both developed and developing countries to combat the adverse impacts of the pandemic due to both health and financial crises, the funding gaps for meeting the SDGs in both water and sanitation sectors will increase very significantly in all counties of the world.

According to the UN Secretary General's latest report (UN, 2020), the situation in many parts of the world is bleak. The report claims that 2.2 billion people around the world do not have "safely managed drinking water", whatever this phrase means. However, if one asks the simple question how many people in the world do not have access to clean and safe water in which they have trust and confidence, it is likely to be at least four billion, more than half the population of the world!

The same UN report (2020) further notes that, in 2017, about 60% of the world's population had basic hand-washing facilities with soap and water at home. However, if the real question is asked, that is, how many people had access to clean and safe water that they trusted, in 2017, the answer has to be that the percentage was most certainly significantly lower, probably well below 50%.

Distressingly this report further noted that, in 2016, 25% of the global healthcare facilities did not have *even* basic water supplies, let alone access to clean and safe water; 20% had no sanitation services; and 40% had no soap and water for hand-washing. Equally, 47% of schools globally did not have handwashing facilities with soap and water. Our experience has been that the UN estimates of such figures, based mostly on data provided by the countries themselves, on various targets of SDGs, have invariably and consistently been overly optimistic. The real situation is much worse.

Clean water is a basic and critical requirement for ensuring the existence of good and functional health services. At least half of the global population currently lacks access to full coverage of essential health services. Clean water is also essential for poverty alleviation, food security, any form of electricity generation and extraction of all minerals, oil or gas.

Global poverty reduction rates were de-accelerating even before COVID-19 became a pandemic. After COVID-19, and based on current evidence, tens of millions of people in the developing world will be pushed back to absolute poverty in 2020 alone. An important exception is likely to be China which now appears to be approaching normal conditions. There is no doubt China will eradicate absolute poverty well before 2025, much earlier than the SDG deadline of 2030.

With climate change, extreme weather events like major floods and droughts as well as large hurricanes and tsunamis are becoming more frequent and severe. All these will affect both developed and developing countries, but efforts to manage such disasters will vary from one country to another. The magnitude of losses will depend on the economic conditions, existence of functional institutions, good governance practices and advanced and effective disaster mitigation and adoption plans.

In 2018 alone, natural and disaster-related costs included 23,458 deaths and 2,064 people went missing, presumed dead. At least 39 million people were affected, and direct economic losses were estimated at $23.6 billion, 73% of which was from the agricultural sector. It should be further noted that major impacts of all natural disasters include lack of availability of clean water and proper sanitation. Unavoidability of clean water and proper sanitation leads to outbreaks of major diseases. These, combined with food insecurity and inadequate nutrition, kill many more people over the short- and medium-term, compared to the disasters themselves.

There is no question that COVID-19 has already contributed to an unprecedented global crisis that has significantly hampered progress in global social and economic development. It has further imperilled progress in terms of achievements of any or all SDGs, including those on water and sanitation. The probabilities of truly reaching the targets of all individual goals were never stellar. COVID-19 has now ensured that it will be a tremendous challenge for the world to reach even a few of these goals.

The British poet Lord Byron wrote a century ago: "Till taught by pain, Men really know not what good water's worth." COVID-19 and numerous deaths earlier due to poor water quality have inflicted enough pain on the world. One can only hope policy-makers finally realise the importance of clean water for everyone and take steps to ensure this happens globally by 2050.

Fig. 9.2. Stockholm Water Awardee Dr Biswas meets Pope Francis.

Fig. 9.3. Buona Sera Dr Tortajada, Third World Centre for Water Management's Co-Founder.

References

Allaire, M., H. Wu and U. Lall (2018). "National Trends in Drinking Water Quality Violations". *Proceedings of the National Academy of Sciences of the United States of America*, 115, no. 9: 2078–2083. <https://doi.org/10.1073/pnas.1719805115>

ASCE (American Society of Civil Engineers) (2017). *2017 Infrastructure Report Card: Drinking Water.* <https://www.infrastructurereportcard.org/cat-item/drinking_water>

AWWA (American Water Works Association) (2019). *2019 State of the Water Industry Report.* <https://www.awwa.org/Portals/0/AWWA/ETS/Resources/2019_STATE%20OF%20THE%20WATER%20INDUSTRY_post.pdf>

AWWA Engineering Modeling Applications Committee (2020). "Water Distribution System Modeling: Past & Present". *Journal AWWA* 112, no. 9: 10–16. <https://doi.org/10.1002/awwa.1572>

Biswas, A. K., ed. (1978). *United Nations Water Conference: Summary and Main Documents.* Oxford: Pergamon Press.

Biswas, A. K. and C. Tortajada (2009). *Impacts of Megaconferences on the Water Sector*. Berlin: Springer.

Biswas, A. K., P. Sachdeva and C. Tortajada (2021). *Phnom Penh Water Story*. Singapore: Springer.

Committee on Oversight and Government Reform (2016). "Examining Federal Administration of the Safe Drinking Water Act in Flint, Michigan, Part 3". <https://oversight.house.gov/sites/democrats.oversight.house.gov/files/documents/Governor%20Snyder%20Testimony.pdf>

Cornwell, D. A., R. A. Brown and S. H. Via (2016). "National Survey of Lead Service Line Occurrence". *Journal AWWA*, 108, no. 4: E182–E191. <https://doi.org/10.5942/jawwa.2016.108.0086>

Corso, P. S., M. H. Kramer, K. A. Blair, D. G. Addiss, J. P. Davis and A. C. Haddix (2003). "Costs of Illness in the 1993 Waterborne *Cryptosporidium* Outbreak, Milwaukee, Wisconsin". *Emerging Infections Diseases*, 9, no. 4: 426–431. <https://dx.doi.org/10.3201/eid0904.020417>

European Parliament (2018*a*). "Drinking Water: New Plans to Improve Tap Water Quality and Cut Plastic Litter". Press Release. <https://www.europarl.europa.eu/news/en/press-room/20181018IPR16523/drinking-water-new-plans-to-improve-tap-water-quality-and-cut-plastic-litter>

European Parliament (2018*b*). "Revision of the Drinking Water Directive / 2018-2". <https://www.europarl.europa.eu/legislative-train/theme-new-boost-for-jobs-growth-and-investment/file-revision-of-the-drinking-water-directive>

European Parliament (2019). "Parliament Supports Plans to Improve Quality of Tap Water and Cut Plastic Litter". Press Release. <https://www.europarl.europa.eu/news/en/press-room/20190321IPR32119/parliament-supports-plans-to-improve-quality-of-tap-water-and-cut-plastic-litter>

Hipel, K. W., N. Z. Zhao and D. M. Kilgour (2003). "Risk Analysis of the Walkerton Drinking Water Crisis". *Canadian Water Resources Journal*, 28, no. 3: 395–419. DOI: 10.4296/cwrj2803395.

Obama White House. (2016). "President Obama Signs Michigan Emergency Declaration". Statements & Releases. <https://obamawhitehouse.archives.gov/the-press-office/2016/01/16/president-obama-signs-michigan-emergency-declaration>

Tortajada, C., Y. Joshi and A. K. Biswas (2013). *The Singapore Water Story: Sustainable Development in an Urban City State*. London: Routledge.

UN (United Nations) (2010). "The Human Right to Water and Sanitation". Resolution adopted by the General Assembly on 28 July 2010 (A/RES/64/292). <https://www.un.org/en/ga/search/view_doc.asp?symbol=A/RES/64/292>

UN (United Nations) 2020. "Progress Towards the Sustainable Development Goals. Report of the Secretary General". <https://sustainabledevelopment.un.org/content/documents/26158Final_SG_SDG_Progress_Report_14052020.pdf>

USEPA (United States Environmental Protection Agency) (1991). "Lead and Copper Rule". <https://www.epa.gov/dwreginfo/lead-and-copper-rule#rule-summary>

USGS (United States Geological Survey) (2009). "Contamination in U.S. Private Wells". <https://www.usgs.gov/special-topic/water-science-school/science/contamination-us-private-wells?qt-science_center_objects=0#qt-science_center_objects>

WHO/UNICEF Joint Monitoring Programme for Water Supply and Sanitation (2012). "Progress on Drinking Water and Sanitation: 2012 Update". Geneva, Switzerland: World Health Organization.

About the Authors

Asit K. Biswas is Distinguished Visiting Professor, University of Glasgow, UK; Chairman, Water Management International Pte Ltd, Singapore; Chief Executive, Third World Centre for Water Management, Mexico.

Cecilia Tortajada is Professor, School of Interdisciplinary Studies, University of Glasgow, and previously Senior Research Fellow, Institute of Water Policy, Lee Kuan Yew School of Public Policy, National University of Singapore.

CHAPTER TEN

IN CONVERSATION WITH LAUREN SORKIN

SHARIFAH HAPSAH

Globalisation, urbanisation and climate change are three global trends that lend urgency to resilience of cities, defined as "the capacity of individuals, communities, institutions, businesses, and systems within a city to survive, adapt, and grow no matter what kinds of chronic stresses and acute shocks they experience".

Cities concentrate risks and as globalisation connects cities more than ever before, a system failure in one city can cause problems across the globe. It is estimated that through urbanisation 68% of the earth's 9 billion people will live in cities and contribute to 80% of global GDP by 2050. Many are in fragile ecosystems with rising debt risks and low real wage growth, with negative impact on disposable income of individuals and families.

Climate change concerns are related to droughts, water shortage, severe weather and floods. (These are further clarified in the authoritative paper on Chapter 9 in Professors Asit and Tortajada's expert views on the state of the developed and developing worlds with respect to the future of clean water and climate change before and after the COVID-19 pandemic.) The most vulnerable are those living in poverty in South Asia, Sub-Saharan Africa, Southeast Asia, Latin America and the Middle East. By 2050, an estimated 800 million people will live in more than 570 coastal cities vulnerable to a sea-level rise of 0.5 meters.

Many cities are already adopting the 12 drivers in the City Reliance Framework covering (a) Leadership and Strategy (Resilience Officers or CROs), often holding senior leadership positions in their cities, and their staff have been trained to embed Urban Resilience principles into city plans, policies, and practices, such as a resilience lens on how they allocate budget or design for the future. Global platform partnerships have also been established to help cities with tools and services in the areas of buildings, governance and policy administration, finance, emergency and disaster management, and Information and Technology.

With regards to the role of universities, case studies in a range of universities around the world have shown that the provision of Training and Education, Technical Expertise and Research have been paramount as expounded in the earlier three volumes on Univer-Cities and their symbiotic relations. Universities prepare the next generation of leaders to solve the urgent challenges of climate change, urbanisation and globalisation through leadership programmes; exchange knowledge to close the academia–policy maker gap, promote investments into resilience infrastructure and collaborate on projects (network and technical expertise).

Reference

Rockefeller Foundation (2015). "City Reliance Framework — 100 Resilient Cities". <https://www.rockefellerfoundation.org/report/city-resilience-framework-2/>

About the Authors

Lauren Sorkin is Acting Executive Director, Global Resilient Cities Network of the Rockefeller Foundation's International Project Study of 100-resilient Cities and Role of Academia in Urban Resilience.

Tan Sri Dr (Med) **Sharifah Hapsah** is Emerita Professor and former Vice Chancellor, Universiti Kebangsaan Malaysia.

CHAPTER ELEVEN

ON STRATEGY FOR DEVELOPING AN INNOVATIVE UNIVERSITY: S-FACTOR, S-GAP AND VECTOR DELTA (δ)

NAM P. SUH

"Young and I were pleased to participate in UC2016 hosted by the University of Newcastle. The concept inveighing universities to create a delta leap to 'transform to leap frog to be on a higher trajectory' has gained credence in these more complex pandemic times. I feel honoured to approve this reprint."

Introduction

Advanced economies need strong research universities. The activities of research universities today affect the future wellbeing of humanity and the world. These universities attract some of the best minds (i.e. students, professors, and researchers) and generate educated human resources to establish and maintain stable, prosperous, and vibrant democratic nations. In addition to generating an educated workforce and future leaders, they advance the knowledge base in science, technology, medicine, biotechnology, economy, transport systems, and many other fields. They also shape the discourse in social sciences, politics, and economics. In addition, they act as incubators and provide homes for technology innovators and future industries. During the last three decades, new relationships among academia, industry, and governments have emerged to involve universities in solving all aspects of societal problems. Universities provide the intellectual fountains that generate and test new ideas. It is easier to have full open debates on disparate and controversial concepts in an academic environment, which provides the long-term stability, progress, and prosperity of society-at-large. Universities have been champions for the free flow of people — professors, researchers, and students — and for thought-provoking ideas. In many countries, universities have provided students with otherwise limited opportunities for upward mobility, which has been important in strengthening democratic society. For these and many other reasons, there is great support for research universities.

During the past six decades, many universities in the world have undergone transformations from purely teaching institutions to research-intensive universities through increased expansion of graduate education and research programmes. The latter seek fundamental knowledge and promote technology innovation. Research universities have attempted to attract specially gifted people from all over the world to their institutions to fill their student ranks, professorships, and research rosters. However, these people tend to favour the better-known research universities in the world. Highly advanced research universities have also attracted more research funds, venture capital, and support of industrial firms because of their reputation and competitiveness. Cities and regions where these research universities are located have attracted capital investments and prospered through the establishment of high technology industries, primarily because of the congregation of outstanding people. Therefore, the race is on to make each research university the most innovative, creative, and productive. Their strive for excellence bodes well for the future of higher education.

Universities have many diverse missions. Central to these missions is the nurturing and education of students as well as providing opportunities for aspiring scholars, and the grooming of future leaders. Some universities do a better job in these tasks than others. Consequently, graduates of competitive universities tend to have more opportunities. Research universities also enhance the culture of technological innovation, the search for fundamental truths in all fields, and enable basic scientific discoveries. All these functions of a research university ultimately contribute to improving the quality of life for all inhabitants of the world. Indeed, the impact made by research universities in creating, discovering, and advancing knowledge through research and education is well recognized in all advanced economies. Because of the important roles of research universities, the quality of universities is of keen interest to prospective students, their parents, funding agencies, and future employers.

Although it cannot be definitively supported by statistical data, the return on investment (ROI) in education and research universities has been substantial. It is most likely that this trend will continue in the future as new knowledge and the people who create new ideas are likely to create new economic engines in many fields for their regions and ultimately for the world. Indeed, exciting things are happening at leading universities in many new fields, as well as in traditional areas of opportunities. For instance, enormous potential exists in established fields such as biotech and medical sciences, information and communications technology, nano-technologies, new materials, artificial intelligence, transportation, energy, water, linguistics, green energy, and energy storage. Even in infrastructure related fields, we need innovations to deal with, for example, the consequences of global warming.

In view of the importance of universities and the strong interest in their quality, several organizations assess and publish relative worldwide university rankings. These rankings are based on two kinds of measures: *quantifiable metrics* and *qualitative measures*. The quantifiable metrics include numerical data on publications, citations, patents, employment of recent graduates, quality of faculty, selectivity of incoming students, financial resources, research funding, and others. On the other hand, the qualitative measures are based on peer reviews, i.e. the opinions of academics and societal leaders about a given university, which is, by its qualitative nature, subjective. Based on these data, these agencies rank universities using unique algorithms. Although some in academic circles dismiss these rankings as frivolous, these rankings nevertheless raise important questions about the responsibility of university administrators in making their institutions more effective and competitive for the sake of their students and the supporters of their institutions.

A few observations about the *top-ranked universities* selected by these ranking agencies may be instructive. First, the top set of universities chosen by many ranking agencies is nearly the same set year after year. The difference in numerical score is small, perhaps within the margin of error. Second, the reputation and known contributions of the top ten universities of the world are clearly discernable without much debate based on their long-standing reputation. However, within any group of 10 or so universities (e.g. those ranked between 45th and 55th), a difference of few points in the numerical score significantly changes their relative rankings. Therefore, the "peer review" — the qualitative part of the assessment — tends to favour well-known universities. If we eliminate the peer review and use only quantitative measures, as was done by Reuters starting in 2015, the list of the "Top Innovative Universities" changes significantly and many well known universities do not make the list. This further supports the fact that the "peer review" favours well-known universities with long histories, i.e. that pedigree matters. Irrespective of the ranking, academicians and academic administrators should be searching for ideas to improve their institutions competitiveness because their students deserve improved education and a more competitive reputation.

Review of Top Ranked Universities by Ranking Organisations

The *Times Higher Education* (THE), a London-based organization, published their top ten highest ranked global universities of 2015–2016 based on their evaluation of teaching, research, knowledge transfer, and international outlook. The top ten universities were then as follows:

California Institute of Technology
University of Oxford
Stanford University
University of Cambridge
MIT
Harvard University
Princeton University
Imperial College London
ETH Zurich
University of Chicago

The names in italics are universities in England, except ETH, which is in Zurich, Switzerland. The rest are all American universities. This list is only slightly different from its 2014 list, which were:

California Institute of Technology
Harvard University

University of Oxford
Stanford University
University of Cambridge
MIT
Princeton University
University of California, Berkeley
Imperial College London & (9) Yale University
University of Chicago

The THE ranked the University of Chicago as 11th because Imperial College and Yale ranked the same 9th place. The important point is that the rank of these top universities hardly changes, although the University of California, Berkeley, did not make the cut in the latest list.

The top 10 highest ranked universities by QS (Quacquarelli Symond, Ltd.), also a London-based ranking organization, is the same as those picked by the *Times Higher Education*, except the order is slightly different as follows:

MIT
Stanford University
Harvard University
University of Cambridge
California Institute of Technology
University of Oxford
University College London
ETH Zurich
Imperial College London
University of Chicago

The universities in italics are again British universities except for ETH Zurich. Again, the same five universities are universities in the United States, but the ordering has changed.

Both the QS and the THE rankings are subjective in that the peer review (i.e. personal views or opinions about specific universities) counts towards the university ranking. A difference of a few points in peer review can drastically change these rankings, especially for lower-ranked universities.

In 2016, Reuters published its 10 *most innovative universities* of the world, which were as follows:

Stanford University
MIT
Harvard University
University of Texas System
University of Washington System
KAIST, Korea
University of Michigan System
University of Pennsylvania
KU Leuven, Belgium
Northwestern University

According to Reuters, the most innovative universities are selected from "the ranks of the educational institutions doing the most to advance science, invent new technologies and help drive the global economy. Unlike other rankings that often rely entirely or in part on subjective surveys, Reuters relies exclusively on empirical data such as patent filings and research paper citations. Our 2016 results show that big breakthroughs — even just one highly influential paper or patent — can drive a university way up the list, but when that discovery fades into the past, so does its ranking. According to our findings, consistency is key, with truly innovative institutions putting out groundbreaking work year after year." <http://www.businessinsider.com/the-2016-ranking-of-the-10-most-innovative-universities-in-the-world-2016-9>

In the Reuters ranking of innovative universities that does not include peer reviews, eight of the ten most innovative universities are in the United States. Three of them (Stanford, MIT, and Harvard) also made the top ten QS and THE lists. The sixth most innovative university in this list is KAIST (Korea Advanced Institute of Science and Technology) of Korea. The ninth is the Katholieke Universiteit (KU) Leuven of Belgium. In this list, none of the British universities make the top ten, whereas in the QS and THE rankings that include peer reviews, half of the top ten are British universities. Reuters chose these universities based on the data on academic papers and patent filings from the Intellectual Property & Science division of Thomson Reuters.

These innovative universities are engaged in the innovation of technologies and the development of socio-economic solutions as well as economic development through the creation of new venture firms. They are also incubators of public policies on issues such as long-term solutions for the environment. Stanford claims that all the companies formed by Stanford entrepreneurs generated US$2.7 trillion in annual revenue, which is equivalent to the 10th largest economy in the world. Similarly, MIT claims that as of 2014, MIT alumni have launched 30,200 active companies, employing roughly 4.6 million people, and generating roughly US$1.9 trillion in annual revenues. That revenue total compares favourably with the world's ninth-largest GDP, Russia (US$2.097 trillion), and the 10th-largest, India (US$1.877 trillion). These two universities, MIT and Stanford, have created not only huge wealth for the United States but also brought many tangible and intangible benefits to people in many other countries.

On the Development of Research Universities

The S-Curve: S-Factor, S-Gap, and Vector Delta

If we define the "S-Factor" as the integrated total measure of the quality of a research university, the development of two research universities over a time period may be depicted as shown in Figure 11.1. This figure assumes a linear change of both A and B, which would be the case when each university works hard to improve through productivity increases and quality improvement. However, the basic assumption may not be valid, because the rate of change, i.e. the improvement of all aspects of a university, may be highly non-linear. The development of a university may be more like the change of the wealth of two individuals, one with much more wealth the other as shown in Figure 11.2.

According to French economist, T. Piketty in his book *Capital in the Twenty-First Century (2013)*, "the rate of capital return in developed countries is persistently greater than the rate of economic growth, and that this will cause wealth inequality in the future". His finding from the historical data in France is that wealth produces more wealth faster than the wealth that can be generated through productivity increases and hard work when the rate of return on capital is greater than the rate of

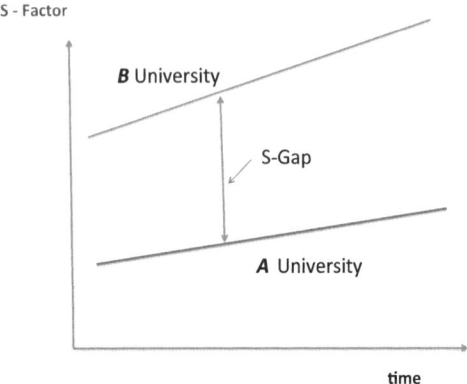

Fig. 11.1. The development of two research universities as a function of time. It shows that university B is developing faster than university A, but both universities are improving linearly as a function of time. The gap between these two universities is denoted as the S-Gap. This change of S-Factor may not be a realistic depiction of what actually happens.

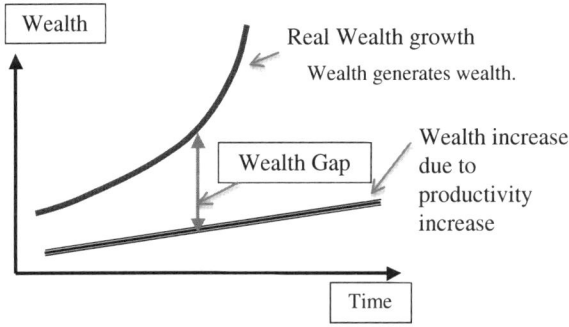

Fig. 11.2. The Piketty curve of wealth growth. The curve on the top shows that the wealthier person gets richer at a much faster rate than the person who tries to accumulate wealth by working harder.

economic growth over the long term. Consequently, rich people (or rich nations) tend to get richer faster because of the wealth that they already possess, i.e. wealth breeds more wealth than just working harder. This finding is schematically shown in Figure 11.2. Similar phenomena may be present in the development of research universities.

A similar phenomenon seems to occur with universities. The universities that are leading in all of their chosen fields have a much greater probability of growing even stronger because of the intellectual, human,

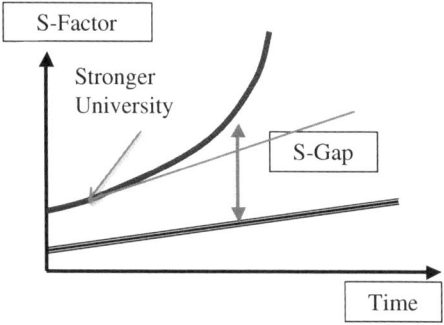

Fig. 11.3. The S-Factor of a university is a composite index of what constitutes the reputation of a university. The lower curve represents a university with a lower S-Factor, which develops more or less linearly with time through hard work, etc. The S-Gap between the wealthier and/or with higher reputation grows by a combination of linear growth and the compound rate due to the existing prior reputation. The S-Gap between these two universities continues to increase unless some drastic actions are taken.

and financial resources that they already have. If we call the aggregation of all the elements that go into strengthening a university the "S-Factor", the growth may be depicted as shown in Figure 11.3. The figure is a composite strength of a university, represented as the S-Factor, as a function of time. The top curve is for a stronger university and the lower curve represents a less well-known university. The stronger university tends to attract better faculty, students, and major financial gifts. Thus, the gap between the two, the "S-Gap", grows as a function of time. The S-Factor is a composite measure made of many elements that make a university great, such as the quality of faculty, students, and staff; the size of the endowment and financial resources; its current reputation; past academic and scholarly achievements; and future prospects. Stronger universities with more "intellectual and financial assets" will grow faster than universities with a low S-Factor. Therefore, the gap between them, the "S-Gap" shown in Figure 11.3, will grow larger with time. For this reason, stronger universities attract more resources and people, which accelerate their growth.

The much faster growth (or advance) of the university with a higher S-Factor is due to many possible factors. The contributing root causes of the S-Gap may be the following:

- More competitive students and faculty go to the universities with better reputations and resources.
- Resources (financial gifts, funds, etc.) tend to concentrate at and/or favour richer universities or better-known universities.
- Faster growth of the S-Factor (e.g. outstanding faculty, students, facilities, reputation, etc.) at stronger universities may be due to the existing advantages.
- Safety factor: for students and faculty members considering their choice of a university, joining a successful enterprise may be deemed safer.
- Quality of life may be better at richer institutions.
- More opportunities may exist at a university with a higher S-Factor.

Vector δ

Universities that have a low S-Factor at a given instant in time (indicated by the lower curve) should not stay on their current trajectory if their long-term goal is to become one of the best universities in the world. They must transition to a higher trajectory as indicated by Vector δ in Figure 11.4. Vector δ may take many different forms depending on specific institutional conditions. For example, Vector δ may consist of the addition of a large number of outstanding faculty members, attracting the most

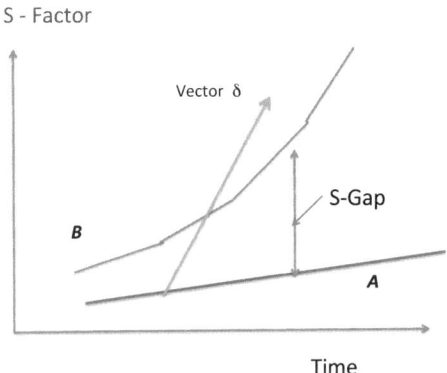

Fig. 11.4. Vector δ to transform University A from its current trajectory to a higher trajectory.

competitive students, generating significant financial resources, making major scientific discoveries, and introducing technological innovations that solve the most important problems of the 21st century. The actions chosen to initiate the transition, i.e. Vector δ, must be achievable goals based on the given conditions of each university. A number of universities (e.g. Arizona State University, Carnegie Mellon University, Georgia Institute of Technology, KAIST, Nanyang Technological University, among others) appear to have gone through transformations to be on a higher trajectory.

Typical characteristics of leading universities often include the following: first, outstanding students and distinguished faculty from all corners of the world want to be at these universities; second, these universities have made major contributions to humanity through major scientific discoveries, technological innovations, and creation of theories of various kinds in all scholarly fields that have changed the way people think; and third, these universities have introduced major educational paradigms that have affected learning and teaching. To create a great university, we must attempt to solve the most profound problems of our era, such as global warming, energy, environment, water, and sustainability. It is easier said than done.

Figure 11.5 shows the impact made by research as a function of the research spectrum, which spans topics from fundamental research to technology innovation. The greatest impact is made by research done at the two ends of the research spectrum, i.e. fundamental research and technology innovation. Yet, most of the research at universities tends to be in the middle of the spectrum, where it is easier to generate results and publish papers. This is because many universities count the number of publications rather than the *impact* made by research as a criterion for promotion and rewards. This is often done because a quantitative measure is much easier to administer than qualitative assessment of the impact made by a faculty member. This is a fundamental flaw at many research universities, because it deprives faculty and students of opportunities for major scholarly and technological contributions by focusing intellectual and financial resources on short-term gains. In reality, the time to generate great ideas and results is not any longer than to work on trivial problems that are hard to publish.

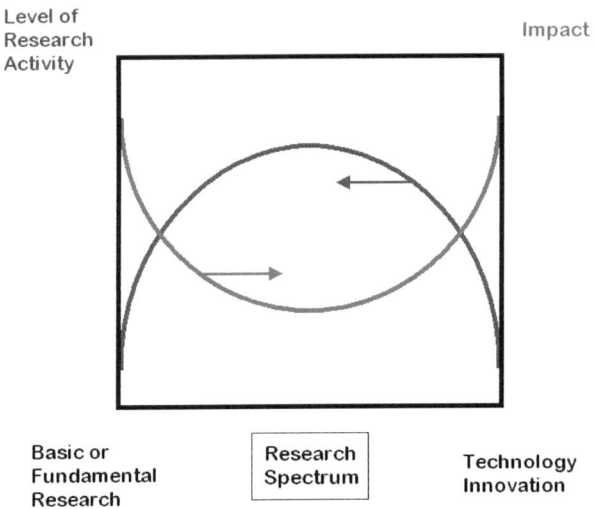

Fig. 11.5. Research spectrum of research done at universities ranges from basic and fundamental research to technology innovation. The level of research indicates the intensity of the research done as a function of research spectrum. Most research is done in the middle of the research spectrum at many universities where the impact (u-shaped curve) made by the research is least. The greatest impact made by research is at either ends of the research spectrum.

Illustration of Vector δ

The KAIST Case

As an illustration of Vector δ, the transformation of KAIST will be briefly reviewed. KAIST was established in 1971 to support the transformation of the Korean economy from labour-intensive businesses (e.g. textiles, apparel, shoe making, etc.) to heavy manufacturing industries for automobiles, steel, ships, electronics, electric power plants, etc. This change was initiated by the Korean Government. To achieve this ambitious goal of industrialisation, Korea needed engineers and scientists with advanced degrees. The Korean Government decided to establish a new university of science and technology, The Korea Advanced Institute of Science (KAIS), that would offer graduate educational programmes in science and engineering rather than investing their scarce resources into then existing universities. It was partially funded by the United States Government through its Agency for International Development (USAID) with a one-time grant. In 1986, KAIS merged with KIT (Korea Institute of Technology), an undergraduate institution in science and technology, to become KAIST. In 2008, it merged again with a small private university in telecommunications (Information and Communications University, ICU).

From its inception, KAIST was given special support by the Korean Government: tuition-free education, higher salaries for the faculty than the then-prevailing salaries at other universities, governance by an independent of board of trustees (rather than by the government ministry), and military deferment for its students once they enrolled in KAIST and successfully completed their education. Since the government controlled the budget and the board of trustees (with four votes out of 18 in 2013), the government had enormous influence over the operation of KAIST. Some of the brightest students in Korea have attended KAIST from the beginning. Many of KAIST's students are the top graduates of special science high schools, which are also highly selective. KAIST has produced a large number of leading engineers and scientists for Korea. These graduates have played key roles in creating the modern industrialised nation that Korea has become. In 2006, KAIST had about 3,000 undergraduates and 5,800 graduate students (now 4,000 undergraduate and 6,500 graduate students), and 400 faculty members (now about 650 professors). About 10% of all professors in Korea in the field of science and engineering are KAIST graduates. The rapid industrialisation and growth of the Korean economy should be attributed to the outstanding work done by able Korean technologists, scientists, technicians, managers, and educators. KAIST graduates have done their part for Korea's industrialisation and also contributed globally by working in many countries.

It should be noted that the Korean economy in 1980 was in dire shape, because the investment made in heavy industries beginning in 1970 had not yet yielded the financial returns. (Investment in heavy industries takes many years to mature.) Also, the new Korean heavy industries had only limited technical know-how and low productivity in the 1970s. In 1980, a major overhaul of the industrial structure was made to increase the competitiveness of Korean companies. By the mid-1980s, the Korean economy was in high gear, ultimately producing the miracle of the Han River.

When I joined KAIST in 2006 as its president, KAIST was a good school with enormous potential but it had a few structural problems. Some of the problems I identified will be outlined here in order to illustrate how KAIST found a new trajectory, i.e. Vector δ. This is an important step since solutions can only be found when the problems are delineated and identified. These problems are not unique to KAIST, but can be found at many universities throughout the world. Nevertheless, it is useful to highlight the problems to provide an integrated view of the issues that had to be resolved.

In 2006, QS ranked KAIST about 196th in the world, a respectable ranking but not certainly where KAIST should be in light of its outstanding students and faculty. KAIST students have been in the top 1% of high school graduates in Korea, many having attended special science high schools and high schools for gifted students. Then what were the reasons it was ranked so low? Clearly, it was not due to problems that individual students or faculty members had created. They were created by the "system" adopted over the years to operate KAIST. This situation may not be unique to KAIST and some other universities may share similar problems.

The basic problems KAIST had can be attributed to malfunctioning of the "system" with unintended consequences. The following issues with students were delineated. Although the majority of KAIST undergraduate students were excellent and studied hard, a small minority of KAIST students took advantage of the largesse provided by Korean people. For instance, KAIST students did not have to perform at their best to graduate from KAIST, since the system allowed them to re-take the same subject until they received the top grade of A. They could also stay at KAIST longer than four years without graduating, still receiving living expenses and free tuition until they graduated.[1] Because of this policy, there were about 800 extra undergraduate students in facilities designed for 3,000 undergraduate students. Since they were exempt from military service, there was no urgency to finish their study in four years. Some of the students, in some ways, were the victims of the Korean secondary educational system. It is extremely competitive to get into (and stay in) good science high schools and high schools for gifted students. Some of KAIST's incoming students were exhausted by the time they graduated from high school. The system did not bring out the best in KAIST students because it did not give them the opportunity to work to their utmost individual capability. These and other problems had to be dealt with to transform KAIST into a merit-based system with intellectual freedom to pursue whatever activity and study the students chose to pursue.

The KAIST graduate school has about **6,500** students, about the same number of students as MIT. The number of graduate students is about 50% larger than the undergraduate programmes at both institutions. However, the number of faculty members at KAIST was much smaller than MIT. (The KAIST faculty was about 40% of the size of the MIT faculty.) Students at KAIST were excellent. However, some doctoral students spent ten years to get a PhD because of the rule that stipulated that doctoral candidates had to have a paper published before they could get their degree. Unfortunately, sometimes, even an excellent paper takes a long time to be accepted and published by a reputable journal. This system persisted, in part because most of the KAIST students received a government stipend administered by KAIST. Therefore, there was no financial burden on the part of either the student or the supervising professor, regardless of the length of their residency at KAIST.[2] Furthermore, since KAIST counted the number of publications rather than quality of the papers and/or innovations for promotion and graduation, many students were working on topics that were similar to those published in the past.

Some aspects of the system for faculty were also lax. Once someone was hired as a faculty member, it was equivalent to getting a lifetime appointment, i.e. almost everyone received tenure. At the same time, even really outstanding faculty members had to wait for their turn for promotion. It was a de-facto seniority-based system, although this was not a part of the formal regulations. The emphasis was on the number of publications rather than the impact made by their research. Since each faculty member supervised a large number of graduate students (whom they did not have to support financially except for those receiving research assistantships) and since all masters and doctoral candidates had to write theses based on research, the number of papers published per faculty was the same as those of world's leading universities in the US, but the impact made by these papers (measured by the number of citations) was much less. In some cases, it was because the papers were refinements of previous papers rather than exploring bold new ideas. Also, the hiring process was not truly objective. It favoured those who were doing work that was similar to the work of others, rather than hiring candidates who had a unique academic background. Almost everything, e.g. lab space, was distributed equally among all professors, regardless of individual needs. Few professors collaborated with other professors in research. Even the most capable and ambitious professors were not able to use their full capability because the system did not recognize and reward exceptional contributions. Their international participation with leading scholars in other countries was limited to a few professors. Thus, the faculty were not competing and collaborating with the best brains of the world. Since the government controlled the size of the faculty, the number of students, budget, physical facilities, etc., there were many problems. For instance, the faculty size was fixed at about 400 and the median age of the faculty was 55 with few professors in their 30s and 40s. In comparison, the size of the faculty at MIT is about 1,000. Since the retirement age was 65, faculty members could not do much once they reach the age of 60, because the system cut back the support for faculty members over 60. By 2006, the buildings and facilities that were built in 1986 had deteriorated for lack of maintenance. Students could not perform research at night and on weekends because the management shut down the heat during the winter. The number of women professors and the international students were miniscule. Instruction was conducted in Korean, sometimes using books translated from English, which limited the global competitiveness of the students. Although this practice can be rationalized from Korean perspectives, this was not consistent with the fact that Korean economy had depended on global trade and overseas markets, and that KAIST graduates were often working for global companies that require proficiency in English. Furthermore, most incoming freshmen were reasonably proficient in English, since many learned it when they were in secondary school.

The Vector δ to change the trajectory of KAIST, which was implemented beginning in 2006, consisted of the following:

1. Decided to increase the faculty size to 700 from 400 unilaterally even without government support. By 2013, the faculty size increased to 630.

2. Adopted a merit-based system for faculty promotion and tenure. Created a super faculty rank of "Distinguished Professor" to reward exceptional faculty members.

3. Evaluated contributions by the impact made in research and teaching, replacing the number of publications.

4. KAIST decided to undertake major research projects to solve global problems of the 21st century in energy, environment, water, and sustainability (EEWS).

5. Created major inter-disciplinary units called KAIST Institutes (KI) by having professors with the same interest share space regardless of their departmental affiliation. Built a large new building that was specifically designed to promote collaboration.

6. A new teaching and learning system was introduced (Education 3.0) where formal lectures were reduced or eliminated and discussion-based teaching through discussion among students with faculty members was favoured to provide the overall guidance and control the contents of the course.

7. Hired faculty members only based on their qualification rather than allocating a fixed number of faculty positions to various departments (a quota system), i.e. departments were allowed to hire as many highly qualified faculty members as they could find. The president of KAIST interviewed all final candidates before the formal offer of employment was made.

8. Adopted English as the language of instruction.

9. Changed the governance system to the department head system, where the department head was responsible for the department decisions on salary, space, and promotion rather than making decisions based on majority faculty vote. The department head controlled the faculty salary based on KAIST-wide policies.

10. Adopted an asymmetric decision-making system. Under this system, the department head could make an affirmative decision on promotion, etc., and then try to get the concurrence of the dean if the dean's approval is needed. If the department head had made a negative decision, the dean and the upper administration could not reverse the department head's decision. The upper administration could render a negative decision, but could not interfere with the decision made by the department head. The philosophy behind this

policy is to empower the department head and let the person who knows more about an issue make the right decision.

11. Increased the number of non-Korean faculty members and international students.
12. Sought an increase in government support.
13. Increased the donations from the private sector.
14. Built 14 new buildings to accommodate increased faculty and student size.
15. Increased the number of undergraduates from 3,000 to 4,000 to increase the number of highly qualified applicants to the KAIST graduate schools.
16. Admission to the KAIST undergraduate programme was based on interviews and high school grades, replacing the written entrance examination.
17. To provide opportunities for students from rural, farming, and fishing villages, 150 students out of 1,000 freshmen were selected for admission purely based the recommendation of the principal of high schools, who were asked to recommend only one student from each school.
18. Increased the number of women faculty and students.
19. Actively promoted international collaboration.
20. Replaced the quantity-based system to a quality-based system in promotion and tenure.
21. Undergraduates who did not finish their degree in four years had to pay tuition.
22. Graduate students who did not finish their PhD in ten years had to pay tuition.

The ranking of KAIST moved up over the following years when these changes were implemented successfully. As stated earlier, by 2016, KAIST ranked 6th among Reuter's most innovative universities in the world. This ranking reflects the fact that KAIST professors and students became much more internationally competitive and influential through their achievements. KAIST professors have won recognitions in international forums and competitions. For example, they won first place at the US Department of Defense competition in robotics. KAIST students obtained easy access to graduate schools in other countries when they chose to study abroad, since the language is no longer a barrier in English-speaking countries. The EEWS programme yielded many major technological innovations such as On-Line Electric Vehicles (OLEVs). OLEVs receive heavy electric power wirelessly from an underground cable, thus eliminating the internal combustion engines from automobiles, buses, etc. KAIST also created the Mobile Harbor (MH). This innovation eliminates the need to build large expensive harbours that damage coastal areas by unloading containers from large ships using a special transport that can easily operate in confined spaces. Also the biological and health sciences became strong by recruiting bright researchers and professors from all corners of the world. The addition of 350 more young professors, increasing the faculty size to 630 by 2013, rejuvenated the faculty rank tremendously.

As Newton's laws state, there is always a "reaction" to any change. This was also the case at KAIST. The Vector δ was implemented at KAIST, although some senior professors, especially those active in the Faculty Association opposed many of these measures. The most resisted changes were teaching in English, the merit-based salary system, and the department head system. There were several reasons for the quick adoption of the new policies, despite the opposition of the Faculty Association. First, the changes were implemented in a relatively short time. Second, the Korean press and people supported the changes. Third, the rapid progress being made under the new system was visible to almost everyone. Finally, the 350 new younger professors who joined the KAIST faculty under the new policies had done outstanding work in research and teaching, and strongly supported these changes.

In retrospect, the behaviour of the KAIST Faculty Association under the leadership of some senior professors was not any worse than the behaviour of those who had lost their privileges. Similar things happened at the US National Science Foundation and at MIT. It must be a human reaction when suddenly one's comfortable life is disturbed by someone's actions, regardless of the long-term benefit of such actions to each individual member of the community, the organization, and ultimately, the nation. Self-interest appears to be the most powerful force that often dictates human instant behaviour. It is sometimes irrational, but it is also perfectly understandable. After all, we are all human beings with our own travails and egos. It is the role of universities to educate people to overcome these negative traits of human being, i.e. for the long-term progress of humanity.

The MIT Case

For four years, I had the privilege of observing engineering research and education conducted at American universities from the vantage of the US National Science Foundation (NSF) as a presidential appointee in charge of engineering. At the time, our goal at NSF was to fulfill the mission of NSF as defined in the NSF Act of 1950 (amended), i.e. to promote advances in science and engineering; provide health, prosperity, and welfare; and secure national defense. We tried to fulfill the original mission of NSF by strengthening the US competitiveness.[3] Although NSF funded some of the best researchers in the country, a large fraction of research funds were granted to well-established senior researchers/professors who were solving similar problems in many different ways under the banner of engineering science rather than working on urgent or new problems so as to advance the engineering field, strengthen the competitiveness of the United States through innovation, and/or solve critical problems of the 21st century. We created many new programmes to support engineering research in fields that lacked the science base (such as design and manufacturing), emerging technologies (e.g. opto-electronics, MEMS, etc.), and critical technologies related to, for example, infrastructure. Another major initiative was the creation of Engineering Research Centers (ERC) to promote interdisciplinary research in universities and in collaboration with industrial firms. We also shifted more funds to support young researchers rather than supporting primarily well-established senior researchers.[4] These changes, including the establishment of the National Earthquake Research Center at the University of New York at Buffalo rather than at one of California' universities, have made me rather unpopular with a certain segment of the higher educational establishments in the United States. However, the University of New York at Buffalo submitted a stronger proposal and the review committee was convinced that the taxpayers money would be better spent there.

One thing I learned was that many grantees did a wonderful job trying to achieve their original research goals, but once the grant money was exhausted, some universities went back to their old system, abandoning the goal of transforming engineering research and education. Based on this experience, I came to the conclusion that it would be difficult to influence the American higher educational system from outside. To make a real change at universities, one has to transform it at the department level from inside the university.

A few years after I returned to MIT from NSF, I was asked to be the Head of the Department of Mechanical Engineering in 1991. I took this job, rather than the presidency of a university, thinking that if the best-ranked department in the field of mechanical engineering changes its direction and programmes, other universities would follow, thus affecting the direction of engineering education and research in the United States, and perhaps even in the world.

My concern with the engineering research in the United States at the time was that after making major progress in many engineering fields after World War II, engineering schools were not working on new problems and issues of the 21st century. Instead, too many professors were solving similar problems many times over, making small incremental improvements rather than spending more time at the two ends of the research spectrum shown in Figure 11.5. By the end of my term at NSF, I realized that the transformation of universities must be attempted from inside a university. The job of being the head of the highest ranked mechanical engineering department in the country was a unique opportunity to achieve this task. Since my professional life had evolved around people who had enormous influence on the development of mechanical engineering at MIT and elsewhere, I thought that I knew how the department could really become great through transformation, which might also help other engineering schools.

The MIT Department of Mechanical Engineering had been the highest ranked department of its kind in the United States, and perhaps one of the best in the world as well. Its faculty members were renowned scholars in various fields of mechanical engineering such as fluid mechanics, heat transfer, solid mechanics, manufacturing, materials, design, and internal combustion. It was indeed a unique privilege for me to learn from the masters of these fields and later to become one of their colleagues. Much of their contributions dealt with issues related to engineering problems that had been created in the late 19th and the first half of the 20th century, which were related to the development of automobiles, electric power plants, mass production, ship building, aerospace, etc. Many of these professors were the best in their respective fields. There were also great scholars at other universities working on similar problems. In fact, in the 1950s under the sponsorship of the Ford Foundation, MIT trained many young engineering professors to increase the supply of engineering professors with PhDs, because many professors did not have advanced degrees. To achieve this goal, brand new PhDs, mostly graduates from MIT, were appointed as "Ford assistant professors" at MIT and taught at MIT for about three or four years. Then they moved on to become faculty members at other universities. These professors and others made American engineering schools to be some of the best in the world, having authored many textbooks, etc. These engineering schools became preeminent in the world in the 1950s and 1960s. Given all these contributions, then the obvious question is: why should the MIT Department of Mechanical Engineering change?

The issue that had to be dealt with in the MIT Department of Mechanical Engineering in 1990s was the transition into new technologies and new problems that are important in the 21st century, and giving up some of the well-established fields in which the professors were well known. It was difficult to go through such a transformation for many reasons. It is always much more comfortable to enjoy the fruits of one's past labour, especially when money was coming in to work on refinements of one's past work. We had the best scholars who led the fields of internal combustion engines, solid mechanics, macro-heat transfer, textiles, machining, and so on. Since most important problems had been solved, many were engaged in the refinement and small advances. To initiate research in new fields, one had to have ideas and perseverance as well as work hard. While we were dwelling on these past issues, new fields were emerging in industry where mechanical engineers could help, if we had developed new tools, theories and methodologies that were applicable to these new problems. For example, in the 1980s, mechanical engineering professors at most universities did not work on problems related to semi-conductor manufacturing, optical devices, micro-device manufacturing, and information science and technology. Heat transfer problems encountered in semiconductor devices required entirely different physics in nano-scale heat generation and transport, which could not be handled based on macro-scale physics of heat generation and transport at nano-scale. Similarly, although the MIT Mechanical Engineering Department led the field of bioengineering, it was done using macroscale mechanical engineering disciplinary knowledge rather than combining that knowledge with knowledge in biology and other fields. We also did not cover optics, which is important in modern manufacturing and mechanical devices. "In-breeding" of the faculty members created some of these problems. Many of the professors in the Department of Mechanical Engineering had received one or more of their engineering degrees from MIT and therefore, the bandwidth of their collective expertise was relatively narrow and often limited to traditional subjects.

During the period 1991–2001, the Vector δ for the Department of Mechanical Engineering at MIT consisted of the following components:

1. Transformation of the discipline of mechanical engineering from a discipline that was largely based on physics to a discipline that incorporates physics, information, biology, and design.
2. Hiring of professors whose background was needed to deal with new issues of the 21st century. As a result, a large number of new professors of mechanical engineering hired did not have their doctorate degrees in mechanical engineering. In 2016, about 50% of the professors in the department had earned their doctorates in fields other than mechanical engineering. They learned about mechanical engineering from their colleagues while teaching mechanical engineering subjects.[5]
3. Stopping the in-breeding of the faculty by hiring most of the new professors from outside.
4. Renovation of physical space to create space to accommodate new research.
5. Emphasis on the two ends of the research spectrum to increase impact made by the research done in the department.

6. Changing the promotion review system to make them more rigorous.
7. Strengthening the interdisciplinary undergraduate mechanical engineering programme (called Course 2A), which increased undergraduate enrollment. In 2016, more than a half of mechanical engineering students were in Course 2A.
8. Strengthened multi-disciplinary research activities.

Challenges in Transforming the MIT ME Department

MIT has a system called the Visiting Committee for each department that gathers information and reports on the state of the department to the MIT Corporation (equivalent to what other universities would call the board of trustees of MIT). The chair of the Visiting Committee is a member of the Corporation. To gather information on the status of the Department, they hold meetings with three groups: tenured professors, un-tenured professors, and students once every one or two years. I think it is a good system.

Four months after I assumed the headship of the department, we had our first Visiting Committee meeting. After the meeting the tenured professors, the chairman of the Visiting Committee came to see me. He told me that 50% of the tenured faculty members voted to ask me to step down from the headship. He suggested that I should leave the headship in four months. I thought of stepping down, but my close colleagues and my wife thought that if I step down, my successors would not dare to make any changes in the future. Six months later when my colleagues saw the results of some of the transformation, they no longer raised this issue again. I stayed in the job for 10 years rather than three years I had originally intended. I give a lot of credit to then MIT President, Dr Charles M. Vest. Instead of asking me to resign, the MIT Corporation changed the chairman of the Visiting Committee. Mr Alex d'Arbeloff became the new chairman of the Visiting Committee, who later became the chairman of the MIT Corporation. Mr d'Arbeloff made many outstanding contributions to MIT and the Department.

After a couple of decades since the transformation, it is good to know that MIT's Mechanical Engineering Department is still ranked No. 1 and stronger than ever. Students are voting with their feet, making it one of the most popular departments to enrol for MIT undergraduates.

Conclusions

The value of having a great university in our midst is well documented. To become such a university, a university may have to transform itself to be on a different trajectory. The transformation should begin with a clear assessment of the factors that have prevented its progress. Based on the assessment, universities must transform to leap frog to be on a higher trajectory. Research universities that dwell only on their past accomplishments will eventually lag behind other universities that continue to leap frog. The trajectory of university development should include discontinuous jumps through timely adoption of innovative changes.

Three concepts are introduced in this chapter: the S-Factor, the S-Gap, and Vector delta. These ideas should solidify the concept of institutional development on a more quantitative basis.

The transformation of KAIST was used to illustrate the multi-faceted aspects of "systems" problems. Today, thanks to the difficult and sometimes painful changes made, KAIST ranks 6th in the world of most innovative universities.

Thanks to the major transformation it has gone through, the MIT Department of Mechanical Engineering continues to be the leading mechanical engineering department in the world.

Universities should strive to become the intellectual hubs where great ideas are created and implemented for public good. The great progress we made in many fields thanks to research at universities gives hope to the idea that we can create an ideal society. The conflicts we see in the world today and the disharmony in many nations that are bringing out the worst instincts of people are ultimately the reasons why our research universities must do a better job to show how a harmonious and just society can and should be created.

Notes

1. Most students at all universities are eager to get higher grades, but the pressure on KAIST students to achieve excellent grades was sometimes greater because of pressure from the students' parents and expectations from society.
2. There are many similarities between KAIST and MIT, but the MIT culture is somewhat different from that of KAIST because the students are responsible

for their tuition, etc. Many MIT graduate students pay their tuition by working as research assistants for professors with research grants.

3. See Dian Olson Belanger, *Enabling American Innovation: Engineering and the National Science Foundation* (West Lafayette, Indiana: Purdue University Press, 1998).

4. Some of these initiatives resulted in the creation of an opposition group called "Concerned Engineers of America", which sent a petition to the White House asking them to dismiss me. About 1,600 people signed it. The letter did not have any effect. I ended up staying in the Washington job for almost four years, although our family had to live on a limited income of a political appointee.

5. We hired new assistant professors based on their educational background, future promise, etc. However, I hired several mid-level professors (i.e. associate professors) from other universities (sometimes by visiting their laboratories to talk to their graduate students at their work) to recruit truly outstanding scholars. They are now leaders of the MIT Mechanical Engineering Department. About a half of them were not in mechanical engineering departments at their previous institutions.

Acknowledgement

The author is grateful to Professor M. Kathryn Thompson for reviewing this paper.

About the Author

Nam P. Suh is Ralph E & Eloise F Cross Professor Emeritus, MIT, Cambridge, MA and Former President, KAIST (2006–2013), Daejeon, Korea.

APPENDIX 1

ADVISORY COUNCIL OF THE UNIVER-CITIES CONFERENCE 2019

Emeritus Professor Bertil Andersson[1]
Nanyang Technological University President and Trustee, Nobel Foundation

Professor Dr Cham Tao Soon, Emeritus Chancellor
SIM University, Founder President of NTU and The Singapore Academy of Engineers. Recipient of the 2006 United Kingdom's Distinguished Engineering International Medal

Former Cambridge Deputy Vice-Chancellor Dr Gordon Johnson
Former President of The Royal Asiatic Society, Deputy Vice Chancellor, University of Cambridge and Chairman, Cambridge University Press

---

[1] Please refer to Appendix 2.

HE Dr Lilia Labidi
Former Fellow, Woodrow Wilson Centre; Visiting Research Professor at the Middle East Institute (National University of Singapore), and Minister for Women's Affairs in the Tunisian cabinet post-Arab Spring

Professor John H McArthur
Dean Emeritus and George F. Baker Professor of Business Administration, Harvard Business School; Duke University Health System Board of Directors; Koç University Board of Overseers; Chairman of Asia Pacific Foundation of Canada; and Officer of the Order of Canada

Emeritus Professor Dr Rudolph A Marcus
John G. Kirkwood and Arthur A. Noyes Professor of Chemistry, California Institute of Technology, Nobel Prize in Chemistry 1992

Tan Sri Dato' Seri Emerita Professor Dr (Med) Sharifah Hapsah Syed Hasan Shahabudin
Former Vice-Chancellor UKM & Senior Consultant, Prime Minister's Department of Malaysia and incumbent President, National Council of Women's Organisation, Malaysia

Emeritus Vice-Chancellor Professor Dr Lap-Chee Tsui

OC, FRS, The University of Hong Kong, discoverer of the gene causing cystic fibrosis and past President of Human Genome Organisation

Emeritus MIT's Ralph & Eloise F Cross Professor Dr Nam-Pyo Suh

Thought leader — Post Fast Proto-typing Innovations at KAIST to the 'Nam-Pyo's Re-Engineered Methodology' to Enhance Probability in Measurable Optimising Completion of Complex Projects to Market

Emeritus Berkeley's Environmental Design Dean & Former Professor of Architecture Professor Richard Bender

Former Dean of the College of Environmental Design and Chair and Professor of Architecture at UC Berkeley. Distinguished place-making from early CERN to CAL and UC System, Mori Foundation to NTU 2010

APPENDIX 2

TESTIMONIUM, AD2017

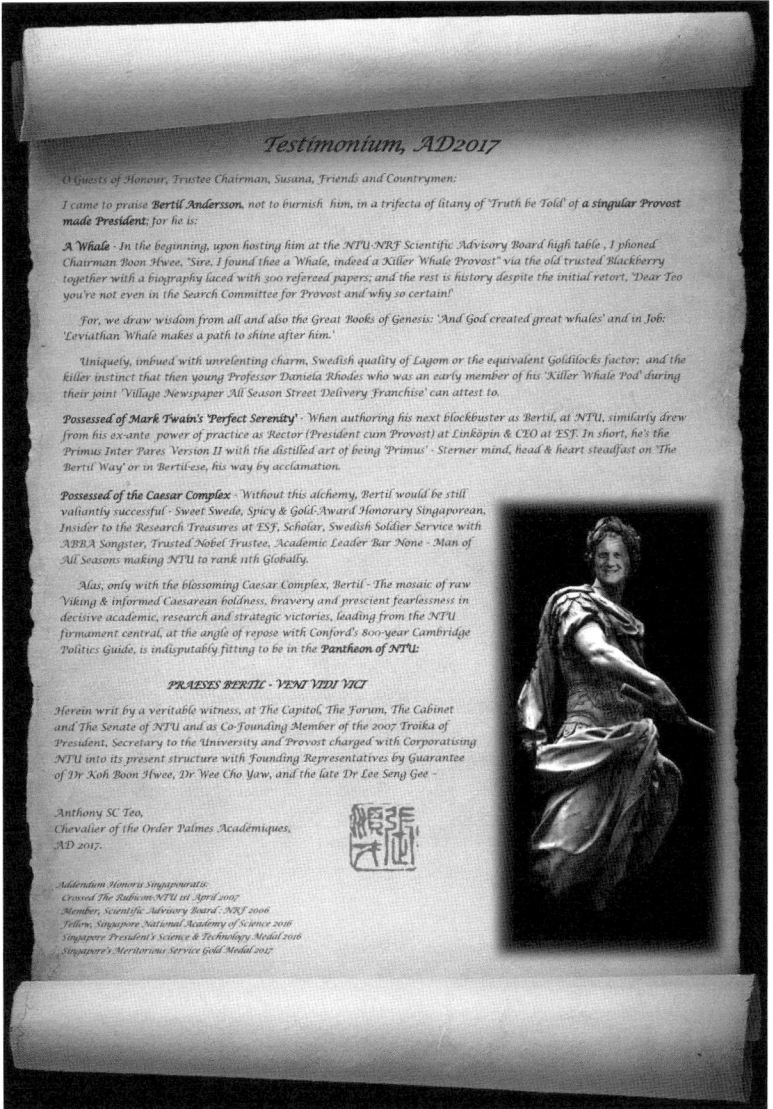

Testimonium, AD2017

O Guests of Honour, Trustee Chairman, Susana, Friends and Countrymen:

I came to praise *Bertil Andersson*, not to burnish him, in a trifecta of litany of 'Truth be Told' of **a singular Provost made President**; for he is:

A Whale - In the beginning, upon hosting him at the NTU-NRF Scientific Advisory Board high table , I phoned Chairman Boon Hwee, "Sire, I found thee a Whale, indeed a Killer Whale Provost" via the old trusted Blackberry together with a biography laced with 300 refereed papers; and the rest is history despite the initial retort, 'Dear Teo you're not even in the Search Committee for Provost and why so certain!'

For, we draw wisdom from all and also the Great Books of Genesis: 'And God created great whales' and in Job: 'Leviathan Whale makes a path to shine after him.'

Uniquely, imbued with unrelenting charm, Swedish quality of Lagom or the equivalent Goldilocks factor; and the killer instinct that then young Professor Daniela Rhodes who was an early member of his 'Killer Whale Pod' during their joint 'Village Newspaper All Season Street Delivery Franchise' can attest to.

Possessed of Mark Twain's 'Perfect Serenity' - When authoring his next blockbuster as Bertil, at NTU, similarly drew from his ex-ante power of practice as Rector (President cum Provost) at Linköpin & CEO at ESF. In short, he's the Primus Inter Pares Version II with the distilled art of being 'Primus' - Sterner mind, head & heart steadfast on 'The Bertil Way' or in Bertil-ese, his way by acclamation.

Possessed of the Caesar Complex - Without this alchemy, Bertil would be still valiantly successful - Sweet Swede, Spicy & Gold-Award Honorary Singaporean, Insider to the Research Treasures at ESF, Scholar, Swedish Soldier Service with ABBA Songster, Trusted Nobel Trustee, Academic Leader Bar None - Man of All Seasons making NTU to rank 11th Globally.

Alas, only with the blossoming Caesar Complex, Bertil - The mosaic of raw Viking & informed Caesarean boldness, bravery and prescient fearlessness in decisive academic, research and strategic victories, leading from the NTU firmament central, at the angle of repose with Conford's 800-year Cambridge Politics Guide, is indisputably fitting to be in the **Pantheon of NTU**:

PRAESES BERTIL - VENI VIDI VICI

Herein writ by a veritable witness, at The Capitol, The Forum, The Cabinet and The Senate of NTU and as Co-Founding Member of the 2007 Troika of President, Secretary to the University and Provost charged with Corporatising NTU into its present structure with Founding Representatives by Guarantee of Dr Koh Boon Hwee, Dr Wee Cho Yaw, and the late Dr Lee Seng Gee -

Anthony SC Teo,
Chevalier of the Order Palmes Académiques,
AD 2017.

Addendum Honoris Singaporatis:
Crossed The Rubicon:NTU 1st April 2007
Member, Scientific Advisory Board : NRF 2008
Fellow, Singapore National Academy of Science 2016
Singapore President's Science & Technology Medal 2016
Singapore's Meritorious Service Gold Medal 2017

APPENDIX 3

ARCHIVAL PHOTOGRAPH USAGE AGREEMENT FOR FIGURE 1.1

ARCHIVAL PHOTOGRAPH USAGE AGREEMENT

Licensor: Lisa Ginsburg
2537 Silver Lake Terrace
Los Angeles CA 90039

Licensee: Anthony SC Teo
Chevalier of the Order Palmes Académiques
Convenor & Editor, Univer-Cities Narrative, Volume I-IV

PROJECT: **National University of Singapore Middle East Institute**
Univer-Cities Conference Publication
"Beating the Odds Together
50 Years of Singapore-Israel Ties"

This agreement between licensor and licensee is **NON-EXCLUSIVE**. The licensee **AGREES TO NOT** enter into separate license agreements with third parties interested in using the same photograph. By this agreement, the licensor allows the licensee present the following **ONE IMAGE at no cost:**

SIR ALBERT EINSTEIN WITH THE FRANKEL-CLUMECK FAMILY
SIR MENASSEH MEYER'S ESTATE, SINGAPORE, NOVEMBER 2, 1922

This usage will be limited to Univer-Cities Conference presentations and publications.

This license is not transferrable to a third party.

LISA GINSBURG remains the sole owner of the image's copyright. No transfer of intellectual property is made by this agreement.

The licensee agrees to credit the licensor, Lisa Ginsburg, in a reasonable manner with this text:

"IMAGE COURTESY OF THE FRANKEL-CLUMECK FAMILY"

This agreement is effective as of **November 30, 2020** and is executed by the undersigned parties representing licensor and licensee.

Lisa Ginsburg
Licensor

Anthony SC Teo
Convenor & Editor, Univer-Cities Narrative
Founding Board Member, NUS MEI
Licensee

LISA GINSBURG • 2537 Silver Lake Terrace, Los Angeles CA 90039
ginsburg10@gmail.com

173

APPENDIX 4

PHOTO CAPTION INFORMATION FOR FIGURE 1.1

PHOTO CAPTION INFORMATION

"Belle Vue," Sir Manasseh Meyer's Estate, Singapore, November 2, 1922

Singapore Jewish Community Reception for Sir Albert Einstein—
Fundraising Event for the Hebrew University in Jerusalem

Einstein's Singapore visit was one part of Einstein's international
fundraising tour for the Hebrew University at the request of World Zionist
Organization president and fellow scientist Chaim Weizmann

BACK ROW FROM LEFT:

(Unidentified man), Mrs. Moselle Nissim, Julian Frankel, Charles R.
Ginsburg, Tila Frankel, Victor Clumeck, Marie Clumeck and Abraham
Frankel

FRONT ROW FROM LEFT:

Alfred Montor, Mrs. Montor, Sir Albert Einstein, Sir Manasseh Meyer, Elsa
Einstein, Mr. Charles Weill, Mrs. Weil and Rosa Frankel

Univer-Cities 2019 delegates at the Singapore University of Social Sciences.

INDEX